MATERIALS FOR LANGUAGE TEACHING AT RUDOLF STEINER (WALDORF) SCHOOLS



# Robin Hood

Retold and annotated by Peter Morris

Illustrated by Christiane Lesch

Pädagogische Forschungsstelle beim Bund der Freien Waldorfschulen

Stuttgart 2005

ISBN-13: 978-3-927286-56-6

ISBN-10: 3-927286-56-7

www.waldorfbuch.de

edition waldorf

## Contents



**THANKS**

Thanks are due to my colleagues at the Engelberg Waldorf School, particularly Bernhard Wolff, for help and advice with the text. And a special thank you to Philomena Beital, copy editor and proof reader *extraordinaire*! Any errors which remain are my own.

*Peter Morris*

# Introduction

## ENGLAND AT THE TIME OF ROBIN HOOD

*Long, long ago, when Richard the Lionheart was King of England, there lived a famous outlaw, and his name was Robin Hood. In those days, the country was much wilder than it is today. There were few towns, and no great roads. Everywhere there were forests, full of deer belonging to the king.*

*King Richard had left England years before to fight in the Holy Land. The land was now ruled by his brother, Prince John, a cruel man who wanted to become king himself. John loved money, and had driven many rich men into the forest as outlaws, so that he could take their land.*

*Poor people suffered even more. Often a penniless father would kill a deer to feed his hungry children. If John's men caught him, they would hang him for this, and so such people had to live in the forests too. Prince John's men grew rich and fat, while King Richard's friends lived as outlaws, hoping that he would soon return to England.*

*One day, news came that King Richard had been made a prisoner on his way back from the Holy Land, but no one knew where he was. Prince John laughed when he heard this. "It's my country now," he said. "My brother will never come home ..."*

## CHAPTER 1

## HOW ROBIN BECAME AN OUTLAW

In the city of Nottingham, near Sherwood Forest, two men were drinking wine in the hall of the castle. Soldiers stood at all the doors, for the two were great men – the Sheriff of Nottingham and Prince John himself, who ruled England while his brother, King Richard, was away.

Prince John laughed. "No, no!" he said. "My brother will never come home. England is mine now!" And the Sheriff of Nottingham laughed with him, happy that Prince John would soon be king.

Suddenly, a man came running into the great hall. The Sheriff jumped up as the man fell on his knees and cried, "My Lords, forgive me! But I have news for you!"

"Tell us, then, fellow!" ordered the Sheriff, looking angrily at the guards who now stood around the man.

"My Lords, I am a servant of Robert Fitzooth, Earl of Huntingdon ..."

"Fitzooth?" broke in Prince John. "But I took away his lands last year! One of *my* men is Earl of Huntingdon now."

"Of course, Sire," said the Sheriff. "But the people here still call him their lord. Go on, fellow!"

"Earl Robert still has a house at Locksley and, in two days' time, he plans to marry Lady Marian Fitzwalter. Tomorrow evening he is going to hold a great feast. If you were to come ..."

"Yes?" said Prince John slowly.

"Then, Sire, you would hear about – Robin Hood!"

"Robin Hood?" Prince John looked at the man in front of him. "I have heard that name. He steals from my friends, does he not, and helps my enemies? And he even kills the deer in my forests!"

"That is true, Lord," the servant said. "He *does* kill the king's deer ..."

"*My* deer, fool!" shouted Prince John. "Tell Sir Guy of Gisborne that we need his help," he said to the Sheriff, more quietly now. "I think we will send him to Fitzooth's feast ..."

Two days later, in the little church by great Sherwood Forest, everything was ready for Robert Fitzooth's wedding. The guests were in their places.

The bride, too, was there, together with her father, Lord Fitzwalter. But where was Earl Robert?

Suddenly, men came into the church. They were dressed in Lincoln green, the colour of the leaves of the forest, and each one carried a longbow over his shoulder. At their head was Earl Robert.

The fat abbot saw the longbows and wanted to protest, but it was too late. Earl Robert's men were already inside the church.

The abbot began. Suddenly horses and loud shouts were heard outside. Then a tall knight came in, and everyone turned round to look.

"I am Sir Guy of Gisborne!" he cried. "His Majesty, Prince John, has ordered me to stop this wedding! His Majesty would like to talk to Earl Robert. Or should I say" – he gave a thin smile – "Robin Hood?"

Turning white, the fat abbot ran out of the church, and many of the guests followed him. Earl Robert spoke proudly.

"Yes," he cried. "I am Robin Hood! And now, until our true king comes back to England, I will leave my house at Locksley and live in the greenwood. Lady Marian – you promised to love me when I was a lord. Will you still have me as an outlaw?"

"Lord or outlaw, I will be your wife!" said Marian proudly.

"My Lord," said Robin to Marian's father, "please take your daughter and keep her safe for me. We have had half a wedding here today, but when King Richard comes back, we shall have a full one!" And turning, he walked out of the church, followed by his men.

"Fitzooth!" Guy of Gisborne's face was hard, and he spoke louder now. "You cannot run! Give me your sword!"

All around Sir Guy, the soldiers held up their spears, but in front of them they saw Robin's men in green. And every man had an arrow ready on his bowstring. The soldiers looked at Sir Guy.

Guy thrust his sword directly at Robin Hood's heart, but Robin stepped to one side. He swung the flat of his own sword to hit Guy's helmet, hard. Sir Guy fell to the ground, stunned.

Without their leader, Guy's soldiers quickly turned to run. Robin's men gave a cheer and then they too were running – into the woods. Soon their Lincoln green had disappeared among the trees. Sir Guy stood up again and shook his head. All he could see was the sun shining on the forest.

*In front of them, they saw Robin's men in green.*

Along secret paths, Robin's men ran deep into the greenwood, till they reached a wide clearing. Here they stopped running. In the middle of the clearing stood the tallest of the forest oaks. Round about, there were caves both deep and dry. Taking his horn from his belt, Robin blew long and loud, and other men dressed in Lincoln green came out of the caves to meet them.

Here in this secret place, the outlaws roasted great pieces of venison over enormous fires. As it grew darker, Robin Hood stood up and spoke to his men.

"We are outlaws," he said. "But not robbers! We will take nothing from poor men, or from women. No one who is good should be afraid of us. But people who are cruel, and hurt others must fear us, for we will fight them till we die, or till King Richard comes home!" The outlaws cheered and cheered.

"Now," cried Robin. "Are you all with me? We will rob the rich and help the poor, till the true king returns!" And there in the forest clearing, the men knelt down together and gave him their promise.

## CHAPTER 2

## HOW LITTLE JOHN JOINED THE OUTLAW BAND

Robin Hood had fine fighting men. But one day he met the man who would become the strongest of all the outlaws. It happened like this.

Robin always wanted to hear what was happening around Sherwood Forest. A rich abbot travelling through the forest, a poor family with no money for food, or an old woman who had been thrown out of her little house – these were things he had to know about. Often he would wander through the forest alone, looking and listening. He knew that, if he blew the big horn at his belt, his men would come to help him as fast as they could.

One morning in summer, he was walking through the forest when he came to a small river. The water looked deep, and Robin did not want to get his feet wet. Then he saw that one of the trees had fallen so that it lay directly across the river, one end on each bank. A fine bridge! As he walked towards it, however, he noticed someone on the other bank moving the same way. It was the biggest man he had ever seen. "Well, I will get to the bridge first," thought Robin, walking more quickly. But the man on the other side moved faster too, and soon both men had reached the bridge. There they stood, one on each side of the river, each with his foot on the tree trunk.

"Move back, Giant!" cried Robin. "I'm going to cross the bridge first!"

"Oh, no, little man!" the giant shouted. "You wait till I've crossed!"

In a flash, Robin had an arrow ready. "Just get off the bridge ..." he said quietly.

"You coward!" shouted the big man. "You stand there with your bow and arrow, while I've only got a quarterstaff!" And he shook the long, heavy stick in his hand at Robin.

"No one calls me a coward!" said Robin, putting his bow on the ground. "Wait – I'll cut myself a staff! Then we'll see who can fight better ..."

The big man smiled. "I'll meet you in the middle of the bridge," he said. "And I hope you like swimming ..."

Quickly, Robin cut a young tree from the forest and took off the leaves. It was about as tall as he was. Soon the two men were standing in the middle of the bridge, with the dark water under them. Suddenly, the giant swung his staff. Robin blocked it, and tried to hit the big man's head. It was a hard blow, but the giant pushed it aside with his staff. Now the heavy sticks swished through the air. After a while, both men were breathing hard, so they rested for a moment. But soon they began again, swinging their heavy sticks till at last Robin lost his balance and fell head-first into the river.

The water was cold, but Robin came up, laughing. Then he saw the giant on the bridge above him. Quickly, his hand moved to the big man's foot and pulled him into the water. *Splash!*

That was the end of the fight. The two men climbed out of the river and sat there together on the tree trunk, both of them wet from head to foot. After a while, Robin took his horn from his belt and, shaking the water from it, blew loud and long. The big man looked at him.

"You fight well," he said.

"You're the best fighter I've ever seen," Robin replied. "Where were you going before we met?"

"I was looking for someone in the forest," said the giant. "People say he's a good fighter too ..."

*They swung their heavy sticks till at last Robin lost his balance.*

At that moment, men in green came running out of the trees. Much, the miller's son, was the first. "Robin!" he cried. "What ... ?"

"Robin?" the big man said slowly. "Not – Robin Hood?"

"Certainly!" said Robin, smiling.

"I was coming to join your band!" cried the giant.

"You will be welcome," said Robin seriously. "Such a fine fighter will be be a great help to us! What's your name, good fellow?"

"John Little," the man replied, his face turning red.

The outlaws roared with laughter. "John *Little*?" cried Much, the miller's son, with tears in his eyes. "That's wonderful! But why don't we just call you – Little John?"

The big man smiled. "Well," he said, "for a new life in the forest, perhaps a new name would be a good idea ..."

## CHAPTER 3

## HOW ROBIN HOOD WON THE SILVER ARROW

A few months later, news came to the greenwood that Prince John and the Sheriff of Nottingham were going to hold an archery contest. The prize would be magnificent – a silver arrow, with feathers of gold!

After dinner that evening, Robin spoke to his men. "I think," he said, "that the men of Sherwood must go to the contest in Nottingham. *We* are the best archers in the country!"

"*You* are the best archer in the country, Robin!" replied Will Scarlett. "But how can you go to Nottingham? Everybody will be watching. Prince John and the Sheriff would love to catch you!"

"Yes," said Robin. "But if I go in disguise, then nobody will know me! It will still be dangerous, so I'll go alone ..."

"Don't talk nonsense, Robin," Little John said firmly. "Of course we'll come with you. And that's that!"

On the day of the contest, the sun shone brightly. Men had come from far and wide to take part, and a long piece of land had been marked out. On one side was the royal stand, where Prince John sat with his friends. On the other side stood hundreds of people who had come to watch. There was loud applause, for the shooting was excellent.

By mid-afternoon, however, only the three best archers were left. One was a King's forester from Delamere, the second came from the Wirral, while the third was a tall man, dressed in the brown hood of a Sherwood forester. A herald stepped forward, calling, "Now the targets will be set at two hundred yards. And each man will have only one shot!"

The forester from Delamere was the first to shoot. Carefully, he drew his bow and fired. A cry went up when the people saw it hit the gold, in the centre of the target. Now the Wirral man stepped forward. He took a deep breath, aimed and fired. The crowd murmured. He too had hit the gold! Then the tall Sherwood man was there, bow in one hand, arrow in the other. He seemed to aim for only a second, then the long arrow hissed through the air. *Gold!* A roar went up from the crowd!

The heralds were seen talking together, then one of them called out to the crowd, "In the middle of the gold ring, we will paint a small, white spot,

*The long arrow hissed through the air. Gold!*

as big as a thumbnail. This is the 'eye', and the man whose arrow comes closest to it will win the contest, and the magnificent silver arrow."

The crowd was very quiet as the Delamere archer slowly drew back his bow and shot. "In the gold, and half in the eye!" came the herald's call, and everyone clapped excitedly.

Now it was the Wirral man's turn. He breathed deeply before taking aim. *Twang – thud!* "Half in the gold, and half in the white of the eye!" came the shout, to cheers from the crowd .

As the tall man from Sherwood walked out in his brown hood, a hard-faced man in the royal stand whispered in Prince John's ear. "Now, Your Majesty, we'll see if our plan has worked!" murmured Guy of Gisborne.

Slowly, the Sherwood man raised his bow and drew. He hardly seemed to take aim, and already his arrow was hissing through the air. *Thud!* The crowd was quiet again, waiting ...

"In the eye! Right in the centre!" came the call. The people of Nottingham cheered wildly, dancing and throwing their hats in the air. The man from Sherwood had won, and now he came forward to take his prize.

He knelt down before Prince John, his face hidden by his brown hood. "Take off your hood when you kneel before His Majesty!" said the Sheriff of Nottingham sharply, and a soldier pulled back the man's hood.

Prince John stood up slowly and turned to the crowd. "I give this silver arrow," he said loudly, "to the best archer of the contest!" Then he looked at the man kneeling in front of him. "What is your name, fellow?" he asked.

"Robert of Huntingdon, Sire," was the reply.

Now Sir Guy spoke. "Perhaps Your Majesty knows this fellow's other name better. It is *Robin Hood!*"

"Robin Hood – the traitor and outlaw?" Prince John smiled. "Your plan has worked, Sir Guy! The silver arrow has brought him to us. Come, guards! We will hang him right here!"

"For shame!" cried Robin. "Is this the prize for the winner?" Sir Guy whispered something in John's ear, and the Prince gave a strange smile.

"You may go, then, fellow," he said. "Soldiers, let him pass!" In a flash, Robin had left the royal stand and disappeared among the crowd.

"Excuse me, Your Majesty," murmured Sir Guy. "I must go to my men. They are waiting for the outlaw ..."

As Robin left the archery field, six of his men joined him. Together, they moved quickly and quietly.

"The contest was a plan to catch me," Robin told the others. "So Sir Guy's soldiers will be waiting for us."

"Be careful, then," said Little John. "They will be right *there*!" In front of them, they saw a group of trees and tall bushes.

"Into the fields!" whispered Robin. "We'll go round them!" The outlaws moved silently through the fields around the trees. They were almost past

*Sir Guy fell backwards out of the saddle and landed in the mud.*

when they heard a shout. Arrows hissed through the air, and they saw soldiers coming towards them. Robin and his men began to run.

The forest was not far away now, but as they ran, they saw more soldiers in front of them – twenty at least. In the middle stood a fine black horse with a hard-faced man on its back – Guy of Gisborne!

*Swish!* Robin heard a low groan at his side. He turned and saw Little John with an arrow in his leg. Robin began to think very quickly. How could they escape?

Suddenly, out of the trees near the soldiers sprang a strange figure in brown robes. It seemed as wide as it was tall, and was swinging a long, heavy stick. Soldiers fell to left and right, and Sir Guy shouted angrily, "Kill him, men! There's only one ..." But as he shouted, a second figure could be seen in the trees. *Swish!* The horse jumped as an arrow hissed past. Sir Guy fell backwards out of the saddle and landed in the mud by the river.

Robin almost shouted with surprise. The archer in the trees, who had frightened Sir Guy's horse, was Lady Marian Fitzwalter!

Guy's soldiers were running now. Quickly, Robin's men picked up Little John and carried him over the bridge. The last of Sir Guy's men threw their master over his horse's back and fled with him.

As the outlaws ran, they were joined by a slim figure in green, with a bow over her shoulder. Lady Marian Fitzwalter had left her home to join Robin in the greenwood – no longer Lady Marian, but Maid Marian of Sherwood! They could not see the man in brown now, and even Marian had no idea who he was. The outlaws scratched their heads and wondered who on earth their helper could be.

## CHAPTER 4

## THE COMING OF FRIAR TUCK

It was autumn now, and life was good in Sherwood Forest. The outlaws held contests in running, jumping, sword-fighting and, of course, archery.

"Who can hit a deer from two hundred and fifty yards?" cried Robin. Little John, whose leg was better now, was the only one who could do it.

"You're the best fighter in England, Little John!" said Robin Hood.

"Except for you, Robin!" replied Little John, smiling.

"Oh, no," said Robin. "Don't you remember how you knocked me into the river?"

"There's one man," said Will Scarlett, "who might beat both of you ..."

"Who's that, Will?" asked Little John.

"He lives on the other side of the forest. He's a friar, a big, fat fellow – you'd think he never stopped eating! But he's one of the best fighting men I've ever seen."

"That's a fellow I must meet! Where does he live?" asked Robin eagerly.

"Well, he *was* a monk at Eastwood Abbey," Will Scarlett replied. "But the abbot threw him out for fighting. So now he lives alone and carries people across the river on his back. He's called Friar Tuck."

So the next morning , Robin went off through the forest. He was thinking hard. Who was the man in brown, who had helped them against Guy of Gisborne. Could he perhaps be this friar? Surely not!

After some time, Robin reached a wide river at the edge of the greenwood. Looking up and down, he could see no bridge. There was only a monk in brown robes, walking along the river bank. He was almost as tall as Robin, and seemed as wide as he was tall. He was wearing a sword at his side and a big, heavy shield was lying on the ground nearby. Robin smiled. Was Will Scarlett right – a fighting monk?

Robin came out of the trees, whistling, and walked up to the man. "Good morning, Friar!" he said cheerfully. "I'd like to cross the river, but I don't want to get my feet wet. So be a good fellow, and take me across on your back, will you? Otherwise ..." He put his hand on the sword at his side.

The monk said nothing, and Robin got up on his back. Slowly, the fat man walked out into the water, which came up over his knees, and crossed to the other bank. There he set Robin down, and spoke his first words.

"Well, here you are! But, you see, I still want to be on the other side. So just carry me back, will you? Or ..." And, putting his hand on the sword at his side, he looked hard at Robin.

The fat friar was even heavier than he looked and, as he crossed back over the river, Robin almost fell. When he reached the forest side of the river, Robin set the man down, panting.

"Thank you very much!" said the monk. "Goodbye!" He turned away, whistling softly to himself.

"I'm terribly sorry!" Robin spoke again. "But now I'm back where I started! So, if you have a moment ..." He put his hand on his sword as he looked deep into the man's eyes. What would the friar say now?

The friar turned patiently, letting Robin get up on his back, and Robin wondered if he was bothering the wrong person. But in the middle of the river, the friar turned suddenly and Robin fell head-first into the cold water. Without a word, the friar walked back to the bank he had come from. Wet from head to foot, Robin was soon on the other bank. He took his bow and shouted, "Come over here, Friar!" But the fat man sprang towards the shield on the grass nearby. Robin fired his arrow, aiming it to frighten the monk. But the man swung his shield and caught the shot in the middle.

"Shoot all your arrows, if you like!" cried the fat man.

Robin was angry. He shot twelve arrows very fast at the man, but the fat friar caught all the shots, till the shield was full of arrows. Robin sprang into the water and crossed over quickly. Now a real fight began, and the river bank rang with the sound of swords. Robin thrust high and low, but the friar did not move one step backwards. After an hour, the fat man was still fighting hard, and Robin's sword felt heavy in his hand.

"Good Friar," said Robin. "Let's rest for a while. May I blow my horn?"

"Certainly!" replied the friar. "Blow till you burst!"

So Robin blew his horn loud and long, and the two men lay down on the grass to rest. Only a few minutes passed, and men in green came running from the forest.

"Robin!" called Will Scarlett. "What's the matter?"

*"Robin?"* said the fat man. "Then you must be Robin Hood. I thought you must be, when you kept me fighting so long!"

"Well, Friar Tuck," said Robin. "It would be good to have a priest and a fighter like you in Sherwood Forest. Will you come and join us?"

"I've often thought of coming," answered the friar. "But there's just one thing ..." He put his hand on his fat stomach. "What do you eat in the greenwood? And, uh, drink?" He looked worried.

Robin threw back his head and laughed. "I'm sorry, good Friar," he said. "Eating is a real problem for us. There's only venison, you see. Great pieces of roast venison from the king 's deer, day in, day out."

The friar's eyes shone.

*The friar turned suddenly and Robin fell head-first into the cold water.*

"And drinking is terrible!" Robin sighed. "Nothing but fine ale, day after day, week after week, from the hundreds of barrels in our caves ..."

"I'll come! I'll come!" said the friar quickly. "When do we start? *Friar Tuck of Sherwood Forest,*" he murmured. "That's a fine name!"

"Tell me," said Robin. "Was it you, good Friar, who helped us at the bridge some days ago, with your stick?" The friar smiled. "Indeed, indeed," he murmured. "I was just passing, and I saw the fight begin. Twenty against seven! *Hmmph!* I hear that Sir Guy still can't sit down. He hurt his bottom when he fell off his horse!" And Robin and his men went off into the forest, laughing.

## CHAPTER 5

## ROBIN HOOD AND THE BISHOP

One day, Robin heard that the Bishop of Hereford would soon be passing through the forest. This bishop was one of the richest men in England, and a friend of Prince John's. So Robin really wanted to meet him.

When the outlaws reached the place where the bishop would pass, most of them hid among the trees and waited. But six men, including Robin, put on shepherds' clothes and sat down beside the track. They lit a fire, and began to roast a great piece of venison which they had brought with them. Soon there was a delicious smell all around.

Now the *clip-clop* of horses' hooves was heard, and the outlaws saw a group of riders. In the middle was the bishop, on a fine white horse, while to the left and right of him, soldiers looked around nervously.

Seeing the 'shepherds', the bishop gave the signal to stop. "What are you doing?" he asked loudly. Then he smelt the meat and broke off. "But that's – venison! The king's deer! The Sheriff will hang you for this, fellows!"

The 'shepherds' jumped to their feet, looking very frightened. "Mercy, Master, please!" cried Robin. "Have mercy on poor men who only wanted to feed their hungry children!"

"Mercy? Nonsense!" said the bishop. "Come on, men! We'll take them to the Sheriff, and he can hang them!"

"Oh, no!" moaned one of the 'shepherds' as the soldiers got off their horses. "Pardon a poor shepherd who – "

*"The Sheriff will hang you for this!" said the bishop loudly.*

"No pardon for you!" said the bishop sharply. "Bind them, men!"

At this, the 'shepherd' took a horn from his belt and blew it. In seconds, the trees were full of men in Lincoln green, each with a longbow in his hand. The soldiers jumped back into their saddles and galloped off, leaving the bishop alone on his horse, with grinning outlaws all around him.

"The bishop wants to have us hanged," Robin told them.

"The bishop? Surely not!" cried Friar Tuck, shocked.

"Oh, yes! *'Mercy? Nonsense!'* was what he said!"

"Shoot him full of arrows, then!" said Little John.

The bishop's hands were trembling now. "Pardon! Pardon for a – "

"No pardon for you, Lord Bishop!" said Robin sharply.

"Please, please don't kill me!" the bishop moaned.

"Kill you?" said Robin. "Oh, no, Lord Bishop, you must come with us. We'll give you dinner here in Sherwood Forest. But you'll have to pay for it!" And off they went along the secret paths of the forest, while the bishop trembled, too frightened to see where they were going.

During the feast that followed, the outlaws laughed and drank, while the bishop sat miserably, the fine meat like ashes in his mouth. Finally, when the meal was finished, Robin turned to his unwilling guest.

"I'm sorry you've eaten so little, Lord Bishop. Didn't you like the food? Well, never mind! Now it's time for you to pay!"

"How much?" muttered the bishop. "I'm not sure if I've got enough ..."

"Oh, that's no problem, My Lord. Just stand up – we'll help you!" And before the bishop could stop them, the outlaws had opened his saddle-bags. Golden coins rained down onto the grass.

"A good start, Lord Bishop! And now that purse, please – and those bags under your shirt! Oh, and the small bags in your boots, too!"

More and more gold was thrown down, and finally the outlaws began to count it. "A thousand pounds!" cried Little John in triumph.

"Wonderful, Lord Bishop!" said Robin cheerfully. "You *do* have enough money to pay for your dinner!"

"A thousand pounds – for *one* meal?" shouted the Bishop. "I've never heard of such a thing! It's *too* much!"

"Ah – but think how many poor people your money will help!" said Robin in a friendly way. "That will be a great comfort to you, My Lord ..."

"Now he's paid for his dinner, let him sing for us too!" cried a voice.

"Yes! Yes! Let him sing!" shouted the others.

*"Sing?"* The bishop could not believe his ears.

"Oh, yes, Lord Bishop. A Sherwood tradition! We know each other's voices so well, you see. But *your* voice is new!"

"Give us a love song!" called a very small outlaw. And everybody laughed.

The bishop was so shocked that he began to sing. His voice was not very good, but the outlaws clapped loudly when he finished. They were thinking of how the bishop's gold would help the poor.

The next morning, they took the bishop back to the edge of the forest. There they set him on his horse – *backwards!* – and off the animal trotted towards Nottingham. The bishop held his horse's tail tightly and stared miserably, as the outlaws went off into the greenwood, singing.

## CHAPTER 6

## HOW ROBIN HOOD MET THE SHERIFF

Walking alone in the forest one day, Robin Hood was surprised to hear someone whistling. Then out of the trees came a horse and a heavy cart, full of fresh meat. Next to the cart walked a short, red-faced man in a blue apron. He was whistling loudly, but stopped suddenly when he saw Robin.

"Well, well – a butcher, here in Sherwood!" murmured Robin, as the short man looked at him nervously. "Good morning, Friend," said Robin politely. "It's nice to hear music in the forest!"

The butcher's voice trembled. "I was just ... " He stared at Robin. "I was hoping to sell this meat at Nottingham market."

Robin had a sudden idea. "Would you like to sell *me* your meat?" he asked. "I'll give you ten pounds, if you lend me the cart and your clothes as well."

*Ten pounds?* The butcher thought this was a wonderful idea, and lay down under a tree to sleep. Robin put on the little man's clothes, which were rather too small for him. Soon, the old horse was walking slowly off towards Nottingham, with a new voice singing loudly through the trees.

"Fresh meat! Threepence a pound! Fresh meat!" called the butchers from their stands. Nottingham market was full of people looking at all the things

*The Sheriff's wife asked Robin to have dinner with her and the Sheriff.*

for sale and fingering the money in their pockets.

"Fresh meat! A penny a pound!" called Robin in his long apron. Soon the housewives were crowding round his cart. The other butchers stared at him. "Hey, Friend, that's much too cheap!" one of them called. But Robin took no notice. "Fresh, tender meat! Only a penny a pound!"

Among the people round the cart was the Sheriff's wife, who was doing her shopping. She looked at the meat and, finding it both fresh and cheap, bought several pounds of it. By now, Robin had already sold most of his meat, and so he talked politely to her. The Sheriff's wife thought him a fine, good-looking man, and asked him to have dinner with her and the Sheriff. With delight, Robin said he would come. .

At the Sheriff's house that evening, Robin learned that King Richard really *was* a prisoner in Europe. But Prince John was telling everyone that Richard was dead, so that he himself might become king.

Later, the talk turned to the butcher's work. The Sheriff wanted to know if his guest had any cattle to sell.

"Certainly, Lord Sheriff," said Robin. "Would you like to see them?"

"Yes, I would, Friend Butcher," replied the Sheriff. "I'll come with you tomorrow, and if I like your herd, I'll give you a good price."

So the next morning, after a fine breakfast, Robin and the Sheriff set off together. Only two men went with them. At first, the Sheriff seemed cheerful, thinking of the profit he would make. But as they rode deeper into the forest, he grew quieter, his eyes looking nervously to left and right.

"Is it much further?" he asked. "Don't forget the outlaws!"

"Do you mean Robin Hood?" replied Robin. "Yes, he lives here. I have often eaten with his men! And quite near here – "

"You know where he lives?" asked the Sheriff eagerly. "I would pay you well to see his hiding-place!"

At that moment, they came round a bend in the forest track, and saw a great herd of red deer in front of them.

"Here they are!" said Robin proudly. "My cattle!"

The Sheriff licked his lips nervously. "The king's deer?" he muttered.

Robin blew his horn and out of the bushes came a large group of outlaws. Seeing the Sheriff, they grinned and clapped their hands.

"You've brought us a guest, Robin!" cried Little John.

*Robin?* So the Sheriff was right to be nervous!

"Certainly! He says he'll pay to see Robin Hood's hiding-place!"

The Sheriff and his men were blindfolded and led along secret paths to the great clearing. There the outlaws gave them a fine feast, although the Sheriff had little appetite.

Afterwards, they counted the gold in the Sheriff's saddle-bags. It came to five hundred pounds. "Keep it, Robin," said Will Scarlett. "The Sheriff was planning to spend the money here in the forest anyway!" The outlaws laughed loudly as the Sheriff pressed his lips together.

The next morning , the three prisoners were blindfolded again and led back to the Nottingham road. From there, they could easily reach town – on foot, of course, for their horses would stay in the greenwood.

"Don't feel too proud, Robin Hood," said the Sheriff coldly. "One day I'll come against you with every soldier I can find. And that will be the end of you!" His voice spat out the words.

"Come whenever you like, Sheriff," Robin replied quietly. "We'll be ready for you!" And off he went into the forest, to give the horse and cart back to the little butcher.

## CHAPTER 7

## THE RETURN OF THE KING

Long years passed. Now people sang ballads about how the men of Sherwood robbed the rich and helped the poor. All the time, the outlaws hoped that King Richard would return. No one knew where he was. But they knew the Sheriff was planning something. So they were very careful.

One day, Robin Hood was walking through the forest with Little John. At a fork in the track, the two men parted.

Going down the right-hand path, Robin noticed a figure among the trees, in the brown hood of a King's forester. In his hand he held a longbow. In a flash, Robin had an arrow on the string of his own bow.

"Can I help you, stranger?" he called. The stranger turned. "I hope so," he replied in a deep voice. "I'm new here. I want to join Robin Hood."

"Come with me, then," said Robin. "But Robin Hood takes only the best fighters. Can you shoot well?"

"Certainly," said the stranger. "I'll show you. What shall I shoot at?"

"How about that tree stump?" said Robin, pointing.

The stranger sneered. "My friends would laugh at such an easy target!"

"Very well, Friend," said Robin quietly. "I'll make you a Sherwood target."

Putting down his bow, he cut a thin branch with his knife.

The man spoke again, and now his voice was thin. "Robin Hood! Turn around – slowly!" Robin knew the voice well, and the man's hard face. There stood Guy of Gisborne, with his bow aimed at Robin's heart.

"You coward!" said Robin. "Fight me man to man!"

Sir Guy only replied, "You forget that you are an outlaw. I shall shoot you, and then blow my horn to tell the Sheriff that you are dead. But if you like, we can hang you in Nottingham instead!"

"Can you hit me?" cried Robin, and he threw his knife at Sir Guy.

The knife flashed past Guy's ear, and the arrow missed Robin, thudding into a tree. Both men drew their swords, and the fighting began. It did not last long, for Robin was half a second faster than Sir Guy. That was enough, and soon Sir Guy lay dead on the ground.

Robin had little time, for he knew that the Sheriff was near. Quickly he put on Guy's brown hood and pulled it over his face. Then he blew the dead man's horn.

Very soon, he heard the thud of hooves, and suddenly, the clearing was full of men on horseback – the Sheriff and his soldiers. Among them were six of Robin's men, all with their hands tied behind their backs.

"We heard your horn, Sir Guy!" called the Sheriff. "What news?"

"The best," replied Robin in Sir Guy's thin voice. "Robin Hood is dead!" And he pointed to the body lying on the grass.

"How shall we reward you?" cried the excited Sheriff. "Gold? A castle, perhaps? Or would you like –"

"No!" Robin said, still speaking in Sir Guy's voice. "Give me these outlaws instead!"

"They are yours, Sir Guy," said the Sheriff, surprised. "But I ..."

Robin moved quickly behind each of the six outlaws, knife in hand, cutting through the ropes which tied them. "When I whistle, then fight for your lives!" he whispered.

"But what are you doing , Sir Guy?" the Sheriff asked. Robin gave a loud whistle. Then began a fight to remember. The outlaws fought well, but the Sheriff had brought many men with him. Back to back Robin's men stood now, swinging swords taken from the soldiers. Robin put his horn to his lips and blew loud and long. But would help come?

Suddenly, hooves thudded again in the clearing, and a clear voice rang out. "So many men, against seven? No, Friends – that's not fair!"

The Sheriff's men saw a knight in black armour riding towards them on a big black horse. He held a long sword in his hand. The Sheriff was so shocked that he fell off his horse. His men did not want such a difficult fight, so they galloped quickly back to Nottingham. The Sheriff got back into his saddle as fast as he could and followed them.

The black knight rode after them, and the greenwood was quiet again. The outlaws stood there, surprised. Who had their helper been?

A few days later, Robin met a new figure in the forest. The man was dressed as a pilgrim from the Holy Land, but Robin kept his hand on his sword.

"Do you have news of the King?" he asked. "Certainly," said the pilgrim. "If you are friends ..."

"All the men of the forest are friends of the King," said Robin. "Come!"

Sitting around the great oak, the outlaws had a feast. The pilgrim seemed to like his food. After the meal, the men begged for news of the King, but the pilgrim only waved his hand.

"Later! Later! First, let's enjoy ourselves!"

"Well," said Robin, "after a really good meal we usually play *buffets*."

"Buffets?" asked the pilgrim. "How do you play that?"

"It's easy," said Little John. "One of us gives you a blow – a buffet. If you stay on your feet, you can give him a blow in return."

"Fine," said the pilgrim. "Shall we begin?"

The first was Much, the miller's son. With his big fist, he struck the pilgrim as hard as he could. But the pilgrim hardly moved and then, raising his own great arm, he knocked Much off his feet.

The outlaws shouted and clapped as the second man stood up – Will Scarlett. He too struck the pilgrim, but in return, the pilgrim laid Will flat on his back. Robin whistled in surprise.

*"King Richard!" gasped Robin, and the outlaws fell on their knees.*

The outlaws were quiet now. The pilgrim stood still as Little John buffeted him, and then he knocked the huge outlaw to the ground as if his fist had been a hammer. Friar Tuck, too, was sent flying off his feet.

Now all eyes turned to Robin Hood. "Robin," gasped Friar Tuck. "You're our only hope. Strike – for King Richard and the honour of Sherwood!"

Robin's arm swung, and the stranger almost fell. He shook his head slowly, and then raised his own arm ...

*"Robin! Robin!"* Robin opened his eyes slowly and saw his friends' faces looking at him. He was lying flat on his back by the fire, where he had fallen under the stranger's blow. The pilgrim was smiling down at him.

"Well, stranger," said Robin. "You're the strongest of us all, and I hope you will join us. But now – what is the news of King Richard?"

The pilgrim's smile grew wider, and he pulled back his hood. "The news of the King is this," he replied. "I am home!"

"King Richard!" gasped Robin, and the outlaws fell on their knees.

"Yes," said the King. "It is I, King Richard – and I was the black knight in the clearing, too. I have been in England for some time, but I wanted to find out who my real friends were." He made a gesture for the men of Sherwood to sit down again.

"You have been outlaws for a long time, but now I must ask you to leave the forest. I need your help. But first, we have something important to do. Where is Lady Marian Fitzwalter?"

Maid Marian stepped forward. Her face was red.

"Where is your priest?"

Friar Tuck, too, stood up and came forward.

"You promised to have a full wedding when the King returned," said King Richard. Robin and Marian looked at each other, smiling. "So now," said the King, "please begin, good Friar!"

So it was that Robin Hood and Maid Marian were married under the great oak, as King Richard and the outlaws looked on. There was great joy that sunny day in Sherwood Forest. Later, they all marched to Nottingham, with King Richard and Robin at their head. Poor people, and those who were good, all ran out to welcome their coming. Now all the King's enemies would have to leave the land and flee!

# Sherwood

Sherwood in the twilight, is Robin Hood awake?
Grey and ghostly shadows are gliding through the brake,
Shadows of the dappled deer, dreaming of the morn,
Dreaming of a shadowy man that winds a shadowy horn.

Robin Hood is here again: all his merry thieves
Hear a ghostly bugle note shivering through the leaves,
Calling as he used to call, faint and far away,
In Sherwood, in Sherwood, about the break of day.

Softly over Sherwood the south wind blows.
All the heart of England, hid in every rose,
Hears across the greenwood the sunny whisper leap:
*Sherwood in the red dawn, is Robin Hood asleep?*

Hark, the voice of England wakes him as of old
And shattering the silence with a cry of brighter gold,
Bugles in the greenwood echo from the steep:
*Sherwood in the red dawn, is Robin Hood asleep?*

Where the deer are gliding down the shadowy glen,
All across the glades of fern he calls his merry men—
Doublets of the Lincoln green glancing through the May
In Sherwood, in Sherwood, about the break of day.

Calls them and they answer: from aisles of oak and ash
Rings the *Follow! Follow!* and the boughs begin to crash;
Friar Tuck and Little John are riding down together
With quarterstaff and drinking-can and grey goose feather.

*Robin! Robin! Robin!* All his merry thieves
Answer as the bugle-note shivers through the leaves,
Calling as he used to call, faint and far away,
In Sherwood, in Sherwood, about the break of day.

*(Abridged and adapted)* Alfred Noyes (1880–1958)

# The Robin Hood Song

*Chorus:*

*Robin Hood, Robin Hood, riding through the glen,*
*Robin Hood, Robin Hood, with his band of men,*
*Feared by the bad, loved by the good,*
*Robin Hood, Robin Hood, Robin Hood.*

1. He called the greatest archers to a tavern on the green,
They vowed to help the people of the King.
They handled all the trouble on the English country scene,
And still found plenty of time to sing.

*Chorus*

2. He came to Sherwood Forest with a feather in his cap,
A fighter never looking for a fight;
His bow was always ready and he kept his arrows sharp,
He used them to fight for what was right.

*Chorus*

This fast, bouncy song, dating from the early 1950s, provides a nice contrast to the older traditional ballads.

# Robin Hood and the Tanner

1. Bold Arthur went out one summer's morning
   To view the merry greenwood,
   To hunt for the deer that ran here and there
   And there he espied Robin Hood, aye ... *(Repeat last line)*

2. "What fellow are you?" says bold Robin Hood,
   "And what is your business here?"
   Says Arthur, "In brief, you look like a thief.
   I'll warrant you steal the King's deer, aye ..." *(Repeat last line)*

3. Then at it they went, bang and bang,
For fully two hours and more:
Each blow and each swing, they made the grove ring,
They played the game so sure, aye ... *(Repeat last line)*

4. Then bold Robin Hood drew a bugle horn,
And blew it both loudly and shrill.
Directly thereon he spied Little John
Come running down the hill, aye ... *(Repeat last line)*

5. "Oh, what is the matter?" then said Little John,
"You're not doing well," he cried.
Says bold Robin Hood, "Here's a tanner so good,
I'll warrant he's tanning my hide, aye ..." *(Repeat last line)*

6. "If he's such a tanner," says bold Little John,
"This tanner that tans so true,
We'll make no doubt but we'll have a fresh bout,
And see if he tans my hide too, aye ..." *(Repeat last line)*

7. "That thing must not be," says bold Robin Hood,
"For he is a hero bold.
He has the best played and he's mastered his trade,
By no man shall he be controlled, aye ..." *(Repeat last line)*

Here, paralleling the *Friar Tuck* story in this book, is the tale of a young tanner who not only stands up to Robin Hood, but even makes him call for help.

This is a version of one of the oldest ballads (see the famous collection by *Francis James Child*). Robin, as ever, is on the side of fairness, admitting his own defeat and protecting the tired tanner – who would have been instantly recognisable as such by his acid-stained hands – from a new fight with the over-eager Little John.

# Would You Like to Know …

### … MORE ABOUT ROBIN HOOD HIMSELF?

Modern scholars disagree on whether there ever was a *'real'* Robin Hood. Existing documents often point in different directions, and nothing can be proved in the normal sense. Believers in Robin Hood feel that history is on their side, saying that 19th century historians thought Homer's tales of the Greeks and the Trojans were mere myths – until Schliemann uncovered Troy.

The case of King Arthur seems somewhat similar. Up until the 1960s, most serious historians thought that Arthur was just a folktale hero. Since then, archaeological evidence has begun to build a factual basis for the story.

Will our ideas about Robin Hood change too, with new discoveries?

### … MORE ABOUT FORESTS IN ROBIN HOOD'S TIME?

Eight hundred years ago, large parts of England were covered by forests. At that time, a forest was not necessarily heavily wooded, and in fact there were large fields, meadows and even towns inside Sherwood. A forest was any area governed by *forest laws*, and set aside for the King's favourite sport – hunting.

The forest laws said that only the King was allowed to hunt the *'beasts of the forest'* – deer and wild boars. Nobody apart from the King and his friends could carry a bow and arrows in the forest. Dogs had to have their toes clipped to stop them from chasing animals. Anyone who was caught breaking the forest laws was treated very harshly indeed. In most cases, he would be hanged.

Sherwood literally meant "Shire Wood", *shire* meaning *county*. And in the Middle Ages, Sherwood did cover much of Nottinghamshire, being over twenty miles long. Many of the trees in Sherwood are oaks and silver birches. One strange kind of oak is the "blasted" oak. These trees have been ravaged by a fungus disease, but legend has it that they were struck by lightning.

### … MORE ABOUT OUTLAWS?

Anyone who was accused of a crime in the Middle Ages was summoned for trial in a court. If the accused person didn't answer the summons, the judge could declare that he was an outlaw.

This was a terrible punishment. An outlaw was said to have a *wolf's head.* Just as anyone was allowed to kill a wolf on sight, because wolves were dangerous, anyone who saw an outlaw was allowed to kill him. Any goods or land that the outlaw owned were taken away and given to the King. Only the King himself could reverse this punishment.

An outlaw had two ways of staying alive. One was to take sanctuary. This meant sheltering in a church, where nobody was allowed to harm others. But sanctuary only lasted for forty days, and after this the outlaw had to leave the church.

The only other way of staying alive was for the outlaw to go into hiding in a remote place, such as a forest, where few people would be likely to see him.

### ... MORE ABOUT LONGBOWS AND ARCHERY?

In the Middle Ages, the law said that every man in England had to own a weapon so that he could help the King defend the country in wartime. The longbow was the cheapest weapon there was, and also the most deadly. An arrow from a longbow could kill a man in armour from almost two hundred metres away!

Because of this, archers were a very important part of English armies, and every king tried to make sure that his people got enough practice. King Edward the Third (1327–1377) not only made archery practice compulsory every Sunday and Holy Day, but also banned other sports like football and cock-fighting so that there would be no interesting alternatives to tempt people!

### ... MORE ABOUT THE KING'S SHERIFFS?

Early in the Middle Ages, English kings divided the country into *shires*. Today, these are called counties, but the old word still lives on in some names – Cheshire or Yorkshire, for example. In each shire, the King had an important person to do his work and look after his business. This person was the *shire-reeve*, or Sheriff.

The Sheriff did four things for the King:

- ✧ he collected taxes;
- ✧ he made sure that people followed the King's orders;
- ✧ he saw that things were in order at the local law courts;
- ✧ he looked after land which the King owned in the shire.

### ... MORE ABOUT MONKS, FRIARS, ABBOTS AND BISHOPS?

In the Middle Ages, thousands of men and women lived a religious life as monks and nuns in monasteries and convents. Their lives were devoted to four things:

- ✧ prayer and the study of the Bible;
- ✧ daily work, mostly in the gardens and fields around the monastery;
- ✧ helping the poor;
- ✧ giving shelter to travellers.

The larger monasteries were called abbeys, and were headed by an abbot or abbess. The smaller ones – priories – had a prior or prioress at their head.

Friars were not bound to a particular monastery, but wandered through the land, preaching to the people and begging for their food.

Monks, nuns and friars lived very simple lives, having no possessions and no money. They spent all their time in work and prayer.

Abbots and bishops, in contrast, usually came from important families, and often owned lands and a great deal of money. In addition to this, most abbeys had the right to collect *tithes*. This meant that people had to give one tenth of all they produced to the abbey. So many abbeys had large amounts of money and property, and abbots and bishops were often more like rich businessmen than monks. In most of the Robin Hood stories, Robin can be very friendly towards poor priests, while he fights against the bishops and their friends, who side with the rich.

# Books Suggested for Further Reading

## BACKGROUND & CRITICISM

✧ *Robin Hood, His Life and Legend* Bernard Miles (Illustrated by Victor Ambrus)
Rand McNally, Chicago, 1984
*Victor Ambrus is an excellent illustrator, and this book is worth having just for the pictures, quite apart from Lord Miles' interesting commentary.*

✧ *Robin Hood: A Complete Study of the English Outlaw* Stephen Knight
Blackwell: Oxford UK and Cambridge, USA, 1994
(Out of print -- try at libraries!)
*This is the definitive book on the legend. It provides the most comprehensive look at Robin Hood. Knight doesn't believe in a real Robin Hood, but he provides valuable criticism.*

✧ *Robin Hood: An Anthology of Scholarship and Criticism* Stephen Knight (editor)
D.S. Brewer, 1999 ISBN 0-859-91525-5
*This new book brings together major studies of the Robin Hood tradition. It contains a variety of approaches, including theatre and film studies, folklore and children's literature. It is, however, extremely expensive (over £60, even for the paperback edition!), so you may prefer to try your library!*

✧ *Robin Hood (Revised edition, paperback)* James Clarke Holt
Thames and Hudson: London, 1989 ISBN 0-500-27541-6
*In the 1980s and early 1990s, this was considered the definitive work on Robin Hood, focusing on the medieval side of the legend. It's still worth having a look at.*

## CLASSIC VERSIONS OF THE ROBIN HOOD STORY

✧ *Robin Hood and Other Outlaw Tales* Stephen Knight & Thomas Ohlgren (eds.)
Western Michigan University, 2000 (2nd edition)
Paperback ISBN 1-580-44067-3
*This is 700 pages long, filled with ballads, plays, and historical background. Much of this book is online at* THE ROBIN HOOD PROJECT AT THE UNIVERSITY OF ROCHESTER (*http://www.lib.rochester.edu/camelot/rh/rhhome.htm – see:* Internet addresses).

✧ *The Merry Adventures of Robin Hood* Howard Pyle
Dover Publications, Inc. ISBN 0-486-22043-5
*A classic version, often recommended. It first appeared in 1884 and was deliberately old-fashioned in its style even then. Pyle's illustrations are wonderful.*

✧ *Robin Hood* Henry Gilbert
Wordsworth Classics, 1994 ISBN 1-853-26127-0
*This retelling dates from 1912 and it shows in the language. It is a fairly complete version of the story, and has two of the Little People as Robin's closest friends.*

✧ *Robin Hood* Roger Lancelyn Green
Puffin Books, 1995 ISBN 0-140-36700-4
*A good overview of the legends, and one of the best Robin Hood books now available.*

✧ *The Chronicles of Robin Hood* Rosemary Sutcliff
Oxford University Press, 1953 (Currently out of print – try libraries!)
*As with most of Sutcliff's work, this is listed as a children's book, but is excellent reading for adults too. A fine retelling of the Robin Hood legend.*

**MODERN VARIANTS ON THE TALE**

✧ *Bows against the Barons* Geoffrey Trease
Brockhampton Press, 1966 (Currently out of print – try libraries!)
*Written in the thirties, this is a left-wing version of the tale, with Robin as the people's hero, fighting for social justice against the rich oppressors. But it can be read as a well-told adventure story too!*

✧ *The Outlaws of Sherwood* Robin McKinley
Ace Books, 1989 ISBN 0-441-64451-1
*A modern retelling for both young adults and grown-ups. It has some nice twists – for example, Robin is the worst archer of all the Merry Men!*

✧ *The Forest Wife* Theresa Tomlinson
Yearling Books, 1997 ISBN 0-440-41350-8
*A young adult book with a feminist view of the Robin Hood legend, focusing on a young Maid Marian who learns magical healing powers.*

✧ *The Sheriff of Nottingham* Richard Kluger
Penguin USA, 1993 ISBN 0-140-17703-5
*In this adult novel, legend is turned upside-down, and the Sheriff of Nottingham becomes the hero, fighting to keep his honesty in a corrupt city of Nottingham.*

✧ *Sherwood* Parke Godwin
Avon Books, 1992 ISBN 0-380-70995-3
✧ *Robin and the King* Parke Godwin
Avon Books, 1993 ISBN 0-380-70996-1
(Both out of print, but available via libraries or at some second-hand shops)
*Two adult novels that rework the Robin Hood legend by setting it more than a century earlier than usual, in William the Conqueror's time. They feature a sympathetic Sheriff of Nottingham. You get a feel for what the clash between the Saxons and Normans must have been like. The second book is set in both England and France, where Robin lives in exile but still serves the King.*

# For Further Study: Internet Resources

The Internet changes faster than most other things these days, so you will probably have to use your own initiative quite often, particularly if you are using this book some time after it was printed (June 2001).

### *Introductory Sites*

- An excellent site to start you off is "Robin Hood – Bold Outlaw of Barnsdale and Sherwood". It offers a Beginner's Guide, sources and links, as well as a Spotlight of the Month and a Robin Hood Picture Gallery:
  *http://www.geocities.com/puckrobin/rh/*
- This address provides a Robin Hood biography, and sections on Robin's England and the Merry Men:
  *http://benturner.com/robinhood/*
- A nice little site is "Amy's Robin Hood Page". It has sections on Fact or Fiction, Robin in Language and Photos and Drawings, but also offers helpful summaries of the original ballads:
  *http://www.webspan.net/~amunno/rhood.html*
- At Nottinghamshire County Council's website, the "Official Visitors' Guide to Nottinghamshire", you will find some nice introductory pages – Myth or Man, Sherwood Forest, On the Trail of Robin Hood and other material:
  *http://www.robinhood.co.uk/themes/robinhood/index.htm*
- In addition to all the usual sections, "Robin Hood" offers material on geography, characters, living history and research:
  *http://www.cadana.com/robin/*
- "The Outlaw Robin Hood" has lots and lots of graphics and provides a great deal of material on places – The Haunts of Robin Hood, some of them with maps:
  *http://www.juliet33.freeserve.co.uk/*
- The Worldwide Robin Hood Society's site is also worth visiting. There is a Robin Hood Online Shop, too, and you can join the society!
  *http://www.robinhood.ltd.uk/robinhood/index.html*
- "Robin Hood: The Legend of Sherwood" offers a newly-written Robin Hood adventure in the form of a play. You can read the first five scenes online, and meet the characters in the Legend of Sherwood Tour:
  *http://sites.netscape.net/legendofsherwood/home.htm*

### *Scholarly Resources and Texts*

- The best scholarly resource is "The Robin Hood Project" at the University of Rochester. It offers a database of texts, images, bibliographies, and basic information about the Robin Hood stories and other outlaw tales. In all, there is an enormous wealth of material: *http://www.lib.rochester.edu/camelot/rh/rhhome.htm*
- At the following two websites, you can download texts of two classic retellings of the Robin Hood story, those of *Howard Pyle* and *Henry Gilbert* (for details of the normal printed versions, see the list of "Books Suggested for Further Reading"):
  *http://www.digital.library.upenn.edu/webbin/gutbook/lookup?num=964* for the Pyle text and
  *http://www.kellscraft.com/robinhoodcontent.html* for Gilbert's.
- The following site offers the definitive Robin Hood Booklist: *http://www.io.com/~tittle/books/robin-hood.html*

### *Other Websites*

- Teachers may be interested in the website of an American college professor who has put a detailed description of his course, "Robin Hood – Mythic Hero or Real Villain?" online: *http://www.loras.edu/~HIS/faculty/jeby/RH.htm*
- *International Socialism*, the journal of the Socialist Workers' Party, offers a detailed Marxist view of our hero in an online article, "Robin Hood: Earl, Outlaw or Rebel?" You can find it at: *http://www.isj1text.fsnet.co.uk/pubs/isj78/cox.htm*
- Lastly, "Swords 'n' Stuff" is an American firm which sells beautiful replica swords, daggers, shields, armour & chainmail from Medieval, Renaissance, Celtic and Roman times. Products are offered in *battle-ready* and *decorative* versions. A full suit of armour can cost up to five thousand dollars, but it costs nothing to look! There is no printed catalogue – only the web pages, richly illustrated: *http://www.swords-n-stuff.com/*

If you have any problems in finding these sites, then go to one of the following search-engines and enter *Robin Hood* in the SEARCH-field:

| | | |
|---|---|---|
| *www.altavista.com* | *www.askjeeves.com* | *www.excite.com* |
| *www.google.co.uk* | *www.goto.com* | *www.hotbot.lycos.de* |
| *www.mamma.com* | *www.nbci.com* | *www.yahoo.com* |

You will get a long list of results – unfortunately including a great number of archery clubs, pubs and social initiatives for helping the poor. Robin Hood's name, it seems, is even more popular than he himself is!

# Thematic Vocabulary (300 WORDS IN 15 GROUPS)

Short forms used in the list:

| | | | | | |
|---|---|---|---|---|---|
| *s.o.* | – someone | – *jemand* | *etc.* | – and so on | – *und so weiter* |
| *s.th.* | – something | – *etwas* | *h.* | – here | – *hier* |
| *opp.* | – opposite | – *Gegensatz* | *s.* | – | – *sich* |

***The following lists comprise those words most helpful for text work and retellings. Teachers will notice that not all the words form a useful addition to long-term vocabulary at this level.***

## THE OUTLAWS (16)

| | | |
|---|---|---|
| outlaw | An *outlaw* lives where people can't catch him. | Vogelfreier; Bandit |
| forest | where lots of trees grow together | (großer) Wald |
| hiding-place | where you go so that no one can find you | Versteck |
| secret | No one knows this – it is *secret.* | geheim; verborgen |
| ➢ | | |
| bow | thing for shooting arrows | Bogen |
| arrow | This is what you shoot from a bow. | Pfeil |
| to aim | to point a bow, gun *etc.* at s.th. or s.o. | zielen |
| to shoot | The outlaws *shoot* arrows in the forest. | schießen |
| to fire | to shoot | schießen |
| to hit | Robin always *hits* what he shoots at. | treffen (= *nicht verfehlen*) |
| to miss | *opp.* to hit | nicht treffen; verfehlen |
| ➢ | | |
| target | Robin's arrows always hit the *target.* | Ziel(-scheibe) |
| archer | person who shoots a bow | Bogenschütze |
| archery | shooting a bow | Bogenschießen |
| contest | game that people try to win | Wettkampf; Wettbewerb |
| prize | what you give to s.o. who has won a contest | Preis (*den man gewinnt*) |

## THE FOREST (16)

| | | |
|---|---|---|
| forest | where lots of trees grow together | (großer) Wald |
| tree | Apples grow on a *tree.* | Baum |
| leaf, leaves | *Leaves* are green things on flowers and trees. | Blatt, Blätter |
| oak | kind of tree | Eiche |
| clearing | place in the forest with no trees | Lichtung |
| deer | wild animal with horns and long, thin legs | Hirsch; Reh; Rotwild |
| ➢ | | |
| cave | Thousands of years ago people lived in *caves.* | Höhle |
| path | This *path* goes from the road to our house. | Pfad; Weg |
| track | small path or road | Weg |
| bend | curve | Kurve |
| fork | At the *fork*, you must take the road to the left. | Gabelung |
| ➢ | | |
| river | The Amazon and the Nile are both big *rivers.* | Fluss |
| bank | We got out of the boat onto the *bank.* | Ufer |
| bridge | s.th. built over a river *etc.* to let us go over it | Brücke |
| (tree) trunk | the thick part of a tree | (Baum-)Stamm |
| ground | We sat on the *ground* to eat our picnic. | Boden; Erde |

**KINGS, PRINCES & SHERIFFS (10)**

| | | |
|---|---|---|
| king | Everyone has heard the name of *King* Arthur. | König |
| prince | son of a king or queen | Prinz |
| Sheriff | important person who works for the king | Sheriff (Vertreter des Königs in einer Grafschaft) |
| important | The King is an *important* person. | wichtig |
| bishop | important priest | Bischof |
| ➢ | | |
| country | Germany is a *country* in Europe. | Land |
| to belong to | This book is mine – it *belongs to* me. | gehören |
| to rule | to be king or queen of | herrschen über |
| to order | to tell s.o. to do s.th. | befehlen |
| servant | s.o. who works in another person's house | Diener |

**PEOPLE (13)**

| | | |
|---|---|---|
| husband | Mr Smith is Mrs Smith's *husband.* | Ehemann; Mann |
| wife | *opp.* husband | Ehefrau; Frau |
| housewife | wife or mother who looks after a home | Hausfrau |
| to marry | Samuel is going to *marry* my sister. | heiraten |
| bride | woman on the day she marries | Braut |
| guest | person who comes to a party, wedding *etc.* | Gast |
| stranger | s.o. that you don't know | Fremde(r) |
| ➢ | | |
| fellow | man or boy | Kerl |
| friend | All my *friends* came to my party. | Freund(-in) |
| enemy | *opp.* friend | Feind |
| crowd | There was a big *crowd* at the concert. | (Menschen-)Menge |
| to crowd | to all come together | s. drängen; s. scharen |
| everyone | all the people; *opp.* no one | jedermann |

**FIGHTING (29)**

| | | |
|---|---|---|
| castle | big, strong building *(= Gebäude)* made of stone | Schloss |
| soldier | person in an army | Soldat |
| leader | chief person | (An-)Führer |
| knight | Have you heard of King Arthur's *knights*? | Ritter |
| rider | person on a horse | Reiter |
| men on horseback | men riding horses | berittene Männer |
| coward | person who is always afraid | Feigling |
| ➢ | | |
| saddle | seat for a rider on a horse | Sattel |
| helmet | Firemen wear *helmets.* | Helm |
| knife | thing for cutting or fighting | Messer |
| sword | long knife for fighting | Schwert |
| shield | Robin's arrows hit the fat man's *shield.* | Schild |
| spear | long stick with a metal point *(= Spitze)* | Speer |
| bow | thing for shooting arrows | Bogen |
| bowstring | the part of the bow that you pull and then let go | Bogensehne |
| arrow | This is what you shoot from a bow. | Pfeil |

| | | |
|---|---|---|
| quarterstaff | long stick for fighting with | Bauernspiess; Schlagstock |
| fist | Boxers hit each other with their *fists*. | Faust |
| ➢ | | |
| blow | In the fight, he got such a *blow* that he fell down. | Schlag |
| to knock | I *knocked* the glass off the table and it broke. | schlagen; stoßen |
| to hit | 1. She cried when the boy *hit* her. | 1. schlagen |
| | 2. Robin always *hits* what he shoots at. | 2. treffen (= *nicht verfehlen*) |
| to strike | to hit; He *struck* me with a stick. | schlagen |
| to miss | My arrow *missed*, and the deer ran away. | nicht treffen; verfehlen |
| to hurt | Helen *hurt* her leg when she fell. | verletzen; wehtun |
| to beat | I can *beat* my father at tennis. | besiegen; schlagen |
| ➢ | | |
| prisoner | person who is not free | Gefangene(r) |
| to tie | to bind | binden |
| rope | They tied the boat to the tree with a long *rope*. | Seil; Schnur |
| to escape | to get away; to get free | entkommen |

**FEELING (18)**

| | | |
|---|---|---|
| to believe | I couldn't *believe* the story he told us. | glauben |
| to hope | It's my birthday tomorrow. I *hope* it won't rain! | hoffen |
| to want | The horse *wants* an apple – I'll give it one. | wollen |
| to wonder | I don't know that boy – I *wonder* who he is. | s. fragen |
| to smile | The child *smiled* at me, and I *smiled* back. | lächeln |
| to laugh | We all *laughed* when the clown's trousers fell down. | lachen |
| ➢ | | |
| surprise | She got a *surprise* when she heard the news. | Überraschung |
| to be surprised | I *was surprised* that my English test was so good. | überrascht sein |
| to bother | Don't *bother* me with silly questions! | belästigen; stören |
| worried | My mother will be *worried* if I come home late. | besorgt; beunruhigt |
| to be afraid of | *Are* you *afraid of* rats? | Angst haben vor |
| to frighten | Don't shout – you'll *frighten* the baby. | erschrecken |
| ➢ | | |
| shocked | I was *shocked* when I saw what he had done. | entrüstet; empört |
| angry | The teacher was *angry* that the class talked so much. | zornig |
| miserable | The little girl was crying because she was *miserable*. | elend; totunglücklich |
| to tremble | She *trembled* when I shouted at her. | zittern |
| to suffer | The poor people *suffered* when they lost their money. | leiden |
| comfort | s.th. that makes you feel better | Trost |

**TALKING & THINKING (25)**

| | | |
|---|---|---|
| voice | With my *voice*, I can speak and sing. | Stimme |
| to talk | I must *talk* to my father about my pocket money. | reden; s. unterhalten |
| to listen | If you *listen* to the teacher, you will learn better. | zuhören |
| to ask | He *asked* me, "Can you speak English?" | fragen |
| to ask for | Emily *asked* her parents *for* a bicycle. | bitten um |
| to answer | He couldn't *answer* my question. | (be-)antworten |
| to reply | to answer | (be-)antworten |
| ➢ | | |
| to promise | My parents have *promised* to take me to London. | versprechen |

| | | |
|---|---|---|
| to cry | 1. "Help!" he *cried*, when he fell into the river.<br>2. The boy *cried* when his dog died. | 1. rufen;<br>2. weinen |
| to shout | He *shouted* for help. *opp.* to whisper | schreien |
| to whisper | She *whispered* so that she wouldn't wake the baby. | flüstern |
| to cheer | to shout 'Hurray!' or 'Hurrah!' | Hurra rufen; jubeln |
| to murmur | to say s.th. very quietly | murmeln |
| to sigh | The teacher *sighed* when I forgot my homework. | seufzen |
| ➢ | | |
| loudly | "Time to begin!" said the teacher *loudly*. | laut |
| quietly | He spoke so *quietly* that I couldn't hear him. | leise |
| That's that! | That is the end of that! | Damit basta! |
| Excuse me! | Forgive me! | Entschuldigen Sie! |
| What's the matter? | What's wrong? What's the problem? | Was ist los? |
| ➢ | | |
| idea | Some more homework? – No! That's a bad *idea*! | Idee; Gedanke |
| to have no idea | What's 'school' in Chinese? I *have no idea*! | keine Ahnung haben |
| nonsense | It's *nonsense* to say that eggs grow on trees. | Unsinn |
| to remember | *opp.* to forget | s. erinnern an |
| to consider | Will you *consider* my idea? | überlegen; in Betracht ziehen |
| to decide | We've *decided* to go to England this summer. | entscheiden; beschließen |

**LOOKING & SEEING (8)**

| | | |
|---|---|---|
| to look | He *looked* very happy when he saw us. | aussehen |
| to look at | Hey! Just *look at* this! | etwas anschauen |
| to notice | to see | bemerken; beobachten |
| to take no notice of | The old man *took no notice of* us. | nicht beachten |
| to watch | to look at (s.o. or s.th.) for some time | zuschauen |
| to stare | to look for a long time | starren |
| to appear | After the storm, a rainbow *appeared* in the sky. | erscheinen |
| to disappear | The train *disappeared* into the tunnel. | verschwinden |

**DOING THINGS (16)**

| | | |
|---|---|---|
| to get up | 1. The little boy *got up* onto his father's back.<br>2. What time do you *get up* in the morning? | 1. (auf-)steigen<br>2. aufstehen |
| to stay | My sister went out, but I *stayed* at home. | bleiben; verbleiben |
| to show | to let s.o. see s.th. | zeigen |
| to point (at) | "Who is that?" he asked, *pointing at* the new boy. | hindeuten; zeigen (auf) |
| ➢ | | |
| to give | Mother *gave* me a glass of milk. | geben |
| to take away | I *took* the knife *away* from the baby.<br>*(to take, took, taken)* | wegnehmen |
| to put on | *Put on* your coat – it's very cold outside. | anziehen (*Kleidung*) |
| to take off | She came in and *took off* her coat. | ausziehen (*Kleidung*) |
| to pick up | The mother *picked up* the crying baby. | (auf-)heben; (hoch-)heben |
| to carry | The mother *carried* the baby to bed.<br>*(to wear, wore, worn = Kleider tragen!)* | *(in Armen, Händen)* tragen |

➢

| | | |
|---|---|---|
| to move | Don't *move*, or I will shoot! | s. bewegen |
| to push | Help! Someone *pushed* me into the water! | stossen; schieben |
| to pull | The little girl was crying, "Billy *pulled* my hair!" | ziehen; zerren (an) |
| to finish | Have you *finished* your homework? | beenden |
| to clap | We *clapped* when our class won the prize. | klatschen |
| to enjoy oneself | The children all *enjoyed themselves* at the party. | s. amüsieren |

**COMING & GOING (10)**

| | | |
|---|---|---|
| to set off | We must *set off* early in the morning. | aufbrechen |
| to leave, left, left | When do you *leave* home to come to school? | verlassen; weggehen (von) |
| to return | to come back | zurückkehren |
| to travel | He often *travels* by train. | reisen |
| to reach | Phone me when you *reach* London! | erreichen |
| to fetch | I will *fetch* you from the hospital. | (ab-)holen |
| ➢ | | |
| to cross | to go from one side to the other | überqueren |
| to pass | to go by (s.o. or s.th.) | vorbeigehen; vorbeikommen |
| to turn round | She *turned round* to look at the boy behind her. | s. (um-)drehen |
| to follow | Saturday *follows* Friday. | folgen |

**'WHERE' WORDS (14)**

| | | |
|---|---|---|
| place | 1. A school is a *place* where people work and learn.<br>2. Barbara! Go to your *place* and sit down! | 1. Ort<br>2. (Sitz-)Platz |
| town | place with houses, shops, offices *etc.* | Stadt |
| market | Every Saturday is *market* day in our town. | Markt |
| church | Some people go to *church* every Sunday. | Kirche |
| road | Is this the *road* to London? | Straße |
| edge | He fell from the *edge* of the cliff. | Rand |
| ➢ | | |
| next to | My best friend sits *next to* me in class. | neben |
| beside | next to | neben |
| among | The teacher stands *among* the girls and boys. | (mitten) unter; inmitten |
| close to | near | nah |
| nearby | Let's go and see Emily – she lives *nearby*. | in der Nähe |
| past | We couldn't get on the bus because it drove *past*. | vorbei |
| everywhere | People *everywhere* know the name of Robin Hood. | überall |
| far and wide | People came from *far and wide* to see our class play. | weit und breit |

**'WHEN' WORDS (29)**

| | | |
|---|---|---|
| life | Have you lived in England all your *life*? | Leben |
| month | January, February and March are *months*. | Monat |
| spring | *Spring* comes between winter and summer. | Frühling |
| autumn | *Autumn* comes between summer and winter. | Herbst |
| hour | 60 minutes (*lesson = Unterrichtsstunde*) | Stunde |
| today | this day; *Today* is my birthday! | heute |

| | | |
|---|---|---|
| yesterday | the day before today | gestern |
| tomorrow | It's Sunday today, so *tomorrow* will be Monday. | morgen |
| day after day | every day; all the time | Tag für Tag |
| ➢ | | |
| at first | at the beginning | zuerst |
| at last | in the end; after some time | schließlich |
| finally | After a long time, we *finally* found the lost child. | schließlich |
| afterwards | later | nachher |
| ➢ | | |
| soon | I worked fast and *soon* finished my homework. | bald |
| suddenly | *Suddenly*, the door opened and the teacher came in. | plötzlich |
| still | I can't come out – I'm *still* doing my homework. | (immer) noch |
| later | I'm working – can we talk *later*? | später |
| until | She will stay in the class *until* summer. | bis |
| after a while | after a time | nach einiger Zeit |
| ➢ | | |
| (long) ago | Now I am 12. A year *ago*, I was 11. | vor (langer Zeit) |
| always | Why do you *always* get up so late? | immer |
| never | People in the Sahara *never* see snow. | nie; niemals |
| usually | normally; We *usually* go to church on Sundays. | gewöhnlich; normalerweise |
| often | I *often* play with my friends after school. | oft; häufig |
| ➢ | | |
| while | *While* we were having breakfast, the phone rang. | während *(vor Hauptwort)* |
| already | I ran to the bus stop, but the bus had *already* left. | schon |
| in a flash | very quickly | im Nu |
| whenever | Come and see me *whenever* you like. | wann auch immer |
| again | Say it *again* – he didn't hear you. | wieder; nochmal |

**EATING (14)**

| | | |
|---|---|---|
| food | We need *food* and drink to live. | Essen; Nahrung |
| to feed | The mother *feeds* her baby with milk. | ernähren; füttern |
| meat | Hamburgers are made of *meat.* | Fleisch |
| piece | Would you like a *piece* of cake? | Stück |
| deer | wild animal with horns and long, thin legs | Hirsch; Reh; Rotwild |
| venison | meat from a deer | Wildbret; Rehfleisch |
| ➢ | | |
| to light | Please *light* the fire. | anzünden |
| delicious | Mmm – this ice-cream is *delicious*! | köstlich |
| smell | There was a *smell* of cooking from the kitchen. | Geruch |
| to roast | to cook *(meat)* in an oven or on a fire | braten; rösten |
| ➢ | | |
| to try | Have you *tried* this chocolate cake? | versuchen; probieren |
| to pass | Could you *pass* me the butter, please? | reichen; herreichen |
| breakfast | first meal of the day | Frühstück |
| dinner | hot meal in the evening | (warmes) Abendessen |

**DESCRIBING PEOPLE & THINGS (32)**

| | | |
|---|---|---|
| cheerful | happy | fröhlich; munter |
| friendly | The new teacher gave me a *friendly* smile. | freundlich |
| polite | It is *polite* to say "Please" when you ask for s.th. | höflich |
| serious | not playing or making a joke | ernst |
| careful | Be *careful* – there is ice on the road! | vorsichtig |
| patient | The old man was *patient* and waited for the bus. | geduldig |
| ➢ | | |
| good-looking | All the boys in this class are very *good-looking*! | gut aussehend |
| ugly | That man looks very *ugly*. | hässlich |
| excited | I was *excited* when our class won the prize. | (*freudig*) aufgeregt |
| nervous | He was alone in the forest and felt very *nervous*. | nervös |
| ➢ | | |
| safe | Will the baby be *safe*, alone? | sicher; in Sicherheit |
| dangerous | Broken glass is *dangerous*. | gefährlich |
| wet | If you fall into the water, you will get *wet*. | nass |
| dry | Wood will burn if it's *dry*. | trocken |
| expensive | £100 for these shoes? That's too *expensive*! | teuer |
| cheap | *opp.* expensive | billig |
| bright | with a lot of light | hell |
| dark | At night it is *dark*. *Opp.* light | dunkel |
| ➢ | | |
| tall | David is a *tall* boy, but his brother is shorter. | hoch; groß(gewachsen) |
| wide | *opp.* narrow | breit |
| heavy | I can't carry this bag – it's too *heavy*. *Opp.* light | schwer (*von Gewicht*) |
| difficult | *opp.* easy | schwierig |
| a lot of | We spent *a lot of* money in the shop. | viel; viele |
| a few | Can I have *a few* flowers for the table? | ein paar |
| ➢ | | |
| nice | Let's go out – it's a *nice* day for a walk. | nett; schön |
| deep | The water is so *deep* – it's over my head! | tief |
| together | Cathy and Jenny always walk to school *together*. | zusammen |
| alone | After his wife died, he lived *alone*. | alleine |
| colour | Blue, green and red are *colours*. | Farbe |
| ➢ | | |
| dressed | For the party, Max was *dressed* in his best T-shirt. | gekleidet |
| dressed as | in the clothes of | verkleidet als; bekleidet als |
| in disguise | in different clothes, to change how you look | verkleidet |

**USEFUL WORDS (50)**

| | | |
|---|---|---|
| money | With *money*, we pay for things that we buy. | Geld |
| coin | piece of money | Münze |
| purse | small bag where you keep money | Geldbeutel |
| poor | having no money; *opp.* rich | arm |
| pocket | He stood there with his hands in his *pockets*. | Tasche (*Hose, Kleid ...*) |
| bag | She came home with a shopping *bag* full of food. | Beutel; Tasche |
| to spend | 1. Larry has *spent* all his money – he has none left. | 1. ausgeben |
| | 2. We *spent* three weeks in France this summer. | 2. verbringen |
| to buy | Go to the shop and *buy* some milk! | kaufen |

| | | |
|---|---|---|
| to sell | That shop *sells* bread. | verkaufen |
| to pay for s.th. | If you want these shoes, you must *pay for* them. | etwas bezahlen |
| for sale | We are leaving town, so our house is *for sale*. | zu verkaufen |
| ➢ | | |
| everyone | all the people | jedermann |
| everybody | The school is empty – *everybody* has gone home. | jedermann |
| nobody | The school is empty – *nobody*'s here. *Opp.* everybody | niemand; keiner |
| no one | *No one* is with me – I am alone. *Opp.* everyone | niemand; keiner |
| everything | *opp.* nothing | alles |
| each | *Each* boy and girl in the class has a chair. | jeder (einzelne) |
| each other | Ann and Judy write letters to *each other.* | einander |
| nothing | I've spent all my money – now I have *nothing*. | nichts |
| ➢ | | |
| with | Will you come to the ice-cream shop *with* me? | mit |
| without | You can't buy things *without* money! | ohne |
| instead | I don't like potatoes. Could I have rice *instead*? | stattdessen |
| of course | naturally; *Of course* I'll help you. | natürlich |
| otherwise | Walk slowly on the ice, *otherwise* you'll fall. | sonst |
| certainly | of course; naturally | gewiss; sicher(lich) |
| really | What do you *really* want for your birthday? | wirklich |
| enough | There is *enough* chocolate for everyone. | genug |
| ➢ | | |
| only | That class is very small – it has *only* ten children. | nur |
| hardly | She speaks so quietly that I can *hardly* hear her. | kaum |
| like | Sally has a pullover *like* mine. | wie |
| both | the two | beide |
| both ... and ... | Lisa speaks *both* French *and* English. | sowohl ... als auch |
| so | The shop is closed, *so* you can't buy any bread. | deshalb |
| although | *Although* I am tired, I can't stop working. | obwohl |
| ➢ | | |
| quiet | Be *quiet* – the baby is asleep. | still |
| quite | It's *quite* warm today. | ganz |
| rather | When I had finished work, I was *rather* tired. | ziemlich |
| perhaps | *Perhaps* I will see him tomorrow, but I don't know. | vielleicht |
| almost | Two minutes to eight! It's *almost* time for school! | fast; beinahe |
| too | I'm going to the park. – Oh! Can I come *too*? | auch |
| as well | Kathy is learning English, and Latin *as well.* | dazu; außerdem |
| at least | That book will cost *at least* £20. | mindestens; wenigstens |
| ➢ | | |
| to happen | The accident (= *Unfall*) *happened* at 3 o'clock. | geschehen; passieren |
| to wait (for) | We *waited* at the bus stop until the bus came. | warten (auf) |
| to go on | Stop talking and *go on* with your work. | fortfahren; weitermachen |
| to need | We *need* water to live. | brauchen; benötigen |
| to be left | He has spent all his money – there *is* nothing *left*. | übrig bleiben; übrig sein |
| the same | His birthday is *the same* day as mine. *Opp.* different | der/die/dasselbe; der/die/das gleiche |
| if | *If* you stand in the rain, you will get wet. | wenn; falls |
| except for | *Except for* Sunday, he works every day. | außer; abgesehen von |

# Opposites & Word-Pairs

*The following pairs are given whenever one of the words occurs in the text. They appear in text sequence. Some of the words are also included in the* Thematic Vocabulary.

*In contrast to normal opposites, word-pairs are not opposites in the true sense, but words often found together, such as* eat *and* drink, see *and* hear, hungry *and* thirsty. *A few pairs of this kind are also included.*

**INTRODUCTION**
**PAGE 3**

| | | | | | |
|---|---|---|---|---|---|
| famous | ⇔ | unknown | berühmt | ⇔ | unbekannt |
| wild | ⇔ | tame | wild | ⇔ | zahm |
| these | ⇔ | those | diese | ⇔ | jene (*Mehrzahl*) |
| everywhere | ⇔ | nowhere | überall | ⇔ | nirgendwo |
| before | ⇔ | after | bevor; vorher | ⇔ | nachdem; nachher |
| to love | ⇔ | to hate | lieben | ⇔ | hassen |
| rich | ⇔ | poor | reich | ⇔ | arm |
| to take | ⇔ | to give | nehmen | ⇔ | geben |
| fat | ⇔ | thin | dick | ⇔ | dünn |
| friend | ⇔ | enemy (*plural*: enemies) | Freund | ⇔ | Feind |
| true | ⇔ | false | wahr | ⇔ | falsch |
| no one | ⇔ | someone | niemand | ⇔ | jemand |
| brother | ⇔ | sister | Bruder | ⇔ | Schwester |

**CHAPTER 1 – HOW ROBIN BECAME AN OUTLAW**
**PAGE 4**

| | | | | | |
|---|---|---|---|---|---|
| near | ⇔ | far (from) | nahe | ⇔ | weit (von) |
| man (*pl.*: men) | ⇔ | woman (*pl*ural: women) | Mann | ⇔ | Frau |
| to drink | ⇔ | to eat | trinken | ⇔ | essen |
| to stand | ⇔ | to sit | stehen | ⇔ | sitzen |
| never | ⇔ | always | nie(mals) | ⇔ | immer |
| happy | ⇔ | sad | glücklich | ⇔ | traurig |
| up | ⇔ | down | (hin)auf | ⇔ | (hin)unter |
| here | ⇔ | there | hier | ⇔ | da; dort |
| lord | ⇔ | lady (*plural*: ladies) | (feiner) Herr | ⇔ | Dame |
| tomorrow | ⇔ | yesterday | morgen | ⇔ | gestern |
| in front of | ⇔ | behind | vor (*räumlich*) | ⇔ | hinter |
| to shout | ⇔ | to whisper | schreien | ⇔ | flüstern |
| quiet | ⇔ | loud | leise | ⇔ | laut |
| late | ⇔ | early | spät | ⇔ | früh |
| little | ⇔ | big | klein | ⇔ | groß |
| everything | ⇔ | nothing | alles | ⇔ | nichts |

**PAGE 5**

| | | | | | |
|---|---|---|---|---|---|
| bride | ⇔ | bridegroom | Braut | ⇔ | Bräutigam |
| father | ⇔ | mother | Vater | ⇔ | Mutter |
| over | ⇔ | under | über | ⇔ | unter |
| head | ⇔ | foot | Kopf | ⇔ | Fuß |
| to begin | ⇔ | to finish | beginnen | ⇔ | beenden; abschließen |

| | | | | | |
|---|---|---|---|---|---|
| inside | ⇔ | outside | (dr)innen | ⇔ | (dr)außen |
| in | ⇔ | out | hineien; herein | ⇔ | hinaus; heraus |
| tall | ⇔ | short | hochgewachsen | ⇔ | kurz |
| to stop | ⇔ | to start | (an)halten | ⇔ | beginnen |
| to talk | ⇔ | to listen | reden | ⇔ | zuhören |
| out of | ⇔ | into | aus ... heraus | ⇔ | in ... hinein |
| many | ⇔ | few | viele | ⇔ | wenige |
| hard | ⇔ | soft | hart | ⇔ | weich; sanft |
| with | ⇔ | without | mit | ⇔ | ohne |

**PAGE 7**

| | | | | | |
|---|---|---|---|---|---|
| wide | ⇔ | narrow | breit | ⇔ | eng |
| deep | ⇔ | shallow | tief | ⇔ | seicht; untief |
| dry | ⇔ | wet | trocken | ⇔ | nass |
| long | ⇔ | short | lang | ⇔ | kurz |
| dark | ⇔ | light | dunkel | ⇔ | hell |

## CHAPTER 2 – HOW LITTLE JOHN JOINED THE OUTLAW BAND

| | | | | | |
|---|---|---|---|---|---|
| strong | ⇔ | weak | stark | ⇔ | schwach |
| often | ⇔ | seldom | oft | ⇔ | selten |
| fast | ⇔ | slow(ly) | schnell | ⇔ | langsam |
| summer | ⇔ | winter | Sommer | ⇔ | Winter |

**PAGE 8**

| | | | | | |
|---|---|---|---|---|---|
| first | ⇔ | last | erste(-r, -s) | ⇔ | letzte(-r, -s) |
| heavy | ⇔ | light | schwer | ⇔ | leicht (*Gewicht*) |
| better | ⇔ | worse | besser | ⇔ | schlechter |
| to lose | ⇔ | to find | verlieren | ⇔ | finden |
| cold | ⇔ | hot | kalt | ⇔ | heiß |
| to pull | ⇔ | to push | ziehen; zerren | ⇔ | schieben |
| end | ⇔ | beginning; start | Ende; Schluss | ⇔ | Anfang |
| together | ⇔ | alone | zusammen | ⇔ | allein |
| well | ⇔ | badly | gut (*Adverb!*) | ⇔ | schlecht (*Adverb!*) |
| good | ⇔ | bad | gut | ⇔ | schlecht |
| best | ⇔ | worst | beste(-r, -s) | ⇔ | schlechteste(-r, -s) |

**PAGE 10**

| | | | | | |
|---|---|---|---|---|---|
| this | ⇔ | that | diese(-r, -s) | ⇔ | jene(-r, -s) |
| wonderful | ⇔ | terrible | wunderbar | ⇔ | schrecklich |
| new | ⇔ | old | neu | ⇔ | alt |

## CHAPTER 3 – HOW ROBIN HOOD WON THE SILVER ARROW

| | | | | | |
|---|---|---|---|---|---|
| to win | ⇔ | to lose | gewinnen | ⇔ | verlieren |
| dangerous | ⇔ | safe | gefährlich | ⇔ | sicher; in Sicherheit |

**PAGE 11**

| | | | | | |
|---|---|---|---|---|---|
| forward | ⇔ | back | vor; nach vorn | ⇔ | zurück |
| careful | ⇔ | careless | sorgfältig | ⇔ | nachlässig |
| white | ⇔ | black | weiß | ⇔ | schwarz |

**PAGE 12**

| | | | | | |
|---|---|---|---|---|---|
| close to | ⇔ | far from | nahe | ⇔ | weit von |
| closest to | ⇔ | farthest from | am nächsten | ⇔ | am weitesten von |
| excited | ⇔ | calm | aufgeregt | ⇔ | gelassen; ruhig |
| to take off | ⇔ | to put on | ausziehen | ⇔ | anziehen; aufsetzen |

**PAGE 13**

| | | | | | |
|---|---|---|---|---|---|
| silent | ⇔ | noisy | still; lautlos | ⇔ | lärmend |

**PAGE 14**

| | | | | | |
|---|---|---|---|---|---|
| air | ⇔ | water | Luft | ⇔ | Wasser |
| strange | ⇔ | ordinary | seltsam | ⇔ | normal; gewöhnlich |
| to pick up | ⇔ | to put down | aufheben | ⇔ | hinlegen |
| slim | ⇔ | plump | schlank | ⇔ | rundlich; mollig |

**CHAPTER 4 – THE COMING OF FRIAR TUCK**

| | | | | | |
|---|---|---|---|---|---|
| autumn | ⇔ | spring | Herbst | ⇔ | Frühling |
| to hit | ⇔ | to miss | treffen; schlagen | ⇔ | verfehlen |

**PAGE 15**

| | | | | | |
|---|---|---|---|---|---|
| to remember | ⇔ | to forget | s. erinnern an | ⇔ | vergessen |

**PAGE 16**

| | | | | | |
|---|---|---|---|---|---|
| wrong | ⇔ | right | falsch | ⇔ | richtig |
| in the middle | ⇔ | at the edge | in der Mitte | ⇔ | am Rande |
| high | ⇔ | low | hoch | ⇔ | tief; niedrig |
| backwards | ⇔ | forwards | rückwärts | ⇔ | vorwärts |

**CHAPTER 5 – ROBIN HOOD AND THE BISHOP**

**PAGE 18**

| | | | | | |
|---|---|---|---|---|---|
| to light | ⇔ | to put out | anzünden | ⇔ | löschen (*Feuer*) |
| delicious | ⇔ | awful; terrible | lecker | ⇔ | schrecklich |
| hungry | ⇔ | thirsty | hungrig | ⇔ | durstig |

**PAGE 20**

| | | | | | |
|---|---|---|---|---|---|
| full | ⇔ | empty | voll | ⇔ | leer |
| grinning | ⇔ | serious | grinsend | ⇔ | ernst(-haft) |
| miserable | ⇔ | delighted | elend | ⇔ | hoch erfreut |
| cheerful | ⇔ | gloomy | fröhlich | ⇔ | betrübt |

**CHAPTER 6 – HOW ROBIN HOOD MET THE SHERIFF**

**PAGE 21**

| | | | | | |
|---|---|---|---|---|---|
| polite | ⇔ | rude | höflich | ⇔ | grob; unhöflich |
| to sell | ⇔ | to buy | verkaufen | ⇔ | kaufen |
| to lend | ⇔ | to borrow | leihen | ⇔ | ausborgen; entleihen |

**PAGE 23**

| | | | | | |
|---|---|---|---|---|---|
| cheap | ⇔ | expensive | billig | ⇔ | teuer |
| good-looking | ⇔ | ugly | gut aussehend | ⇔ | hässlich |
| dead | ⇔ | alive | tot | ⇔ | lebend |
| next | ⇔ | previous | nächste(-r, -s) | ⇔ | vorherig |
| next week/year | ⇔ | last week/year | nächste Woche; nächstes Jahr | ⇔ | letzte Woche; letztes Jahr |

**CHAPTER 7 – THE RETURN OF THE KING**

**PAGE 25**

| | | | | | |
|---|---|---|---|---|---|
| easy | ⇔ | difficult | leicht | ⇔ | schwierig |

**PAGE 26**

| | | | | | |
|---|---|---|---|---|---|
| to like | ⇔ | to dislike | gern haben | ⇔ | nicht mögen |
| to enjoy oneself | ⇔ | to be bored | s. amüsieren | ⇔ | s. langweilen |

**PAGE 28**

| | | | | | |
|---|---|---|---|---|---|
| important | ⇔ | trivial | wichtig | ⇔ | banal; unwesentlich |
| sunny | ⇔ | cloudy | sonnig | ⇔ | bewölkt |

# Vocabulary Page by Page

☞ *See list of short forms on page 40.*

☞ ***These annotations are intended to help with the text, not to be learned "as is". Those items unnecessary for active vocabulary at this level should be skipped.***

**INTRODUCTION – ENGLAND AT THE TIME OF ROBIN HOOD**

**PAGE 3**

| | | |
|---|---|---|
| introduction | The *introduction* tells you what the book is about. | Einleitung; Einführung |
| (long) ago | Now I am 12. A year *ago*, I was 11. | vor (langer Zeit) |
| Lionheart | *name for* King Richard I of England *(1157–1199)* | Löwenherz |
| famous | Hollywood is *famous* for its films. | berühmt |
| outlaw | An *outlaw* lives in wild places where people can't find him or catch him. | Vogelfreier; Bandit |
| country | land; Italy is a *country* in Europe. | Land |
| today | this day; yesterday, *today* and tomorrow | heute |
| few | *opp.* many | wenige |
| town | place with houses, shops, offices *etc.* | Stadt |
| road | Is this the *road* to London? | Straße |
| everywhere | People *everywhere* know the name of Robin Hood. | überall |
| forest | where lots of trees grow together | (großer) Wald |
| deer | wild animal with horns and long, thin legs | Hirsch; Reh; Rotwild |
| to belong to | This book is mine – it *belongs to* me. | gehören |
| to leave | When do you *leave* home to come to school? (*to leave, left, left*) | verlassen; weggehen (von) |
| Holy Land | Israel | das Heilige Land |
| to rule | to be king or queen of | herrschen |
| cruel | The *cruel* man was hitting the horse. | grausam; hart |
| money | With *money*, we pay for things that we buy. | Geld |
| to drive | *h:* to make s.o. go (*to drive, drove, driven*) | *h:* vertreiben |
| to suffer | My father *suffers* from asthma. | leiden |
| even more | I ate four ice-creams, but my friend ate *even more.* | noch mehr |
| penniless | poor; having no money | mittellos; ganz arm |
| to feed | A mother *feeds* her baby with milk. ( to feed, fed, fed) | ernähren; füttern |
| to hang | *h:* to kill s.o. on a gallows (= *Galgen*) | *h:* hängen (*Galgen*) |
| if | *If* you stand in the rain, you will get wet. | wenn; falls |
| such | I'd love a Rolls-Royce, but *such* cars cost a lot. | solch(-er, -e, -es) |
| too | I'm going to the park. – Oh! Can I come *too*? | auch |
| to grow | *h:* to become (*to grow, grew, grown*) | *h:* werden |
| while | *While* we were having breakfast, the phone rang. | während *(vor Hauptwort)* |
| to hope | It's my birthday tomorrow. I *hope* it won't rain! | hoffen |
| soon | in a short time | bald |
| to return | to come back | zurückkehren |
| news | story about s.th. that has happened | Nachricht(en) |
| prisoner | person who is not free | Gefangene(r) |
| to laugh | We all *laughed* when the clown's trousers fell down. | lachen |
| never | Children in Nigeria *never* see snow. | nie; niemals |

## CHAPTER 1 – HOW ROBIN BECAME AN OUTLAW

### PAGE 4

| | | |
|---|---|---|
| outlaw | An *outlaw* lives in wild places where people can't find him or catch him. | Vogelfreier; Bandit |
| forest | where lots of trees grow together | (großer) Wald |
| hall | *h:* big room | *h:* Saal |
| castle | big, strong building *(= Gebäude)* made of stone | Schloss; Burg |
| soldier | person in an army | Soldat |
| Sheriff | important person who works for the king | Sheriff (Vertreter des Königs in einer Grafschaft) |
| to rule | to be king or queen of | herrschen über |
| to take away | I *took* the knife *away* from the baby. *(to take, took, taken)* | wegnehmen |
| to laugh | All the children *laughed* when the clown's trousers fell down. | lachen |
| soon | in a short time | bald |
| suddenly | I was sleeping when *suddenly*, the teacher spoke. | plötzlich |
| to cry | 1. "Help!" he *cried*, when he fell into the river. 2. The boy *cried* when his dog died. | 1. rufen; 2. weinen |
| news | story about something that has happened | Nachricht(en) |
| fellow | man or boy | Kerl |
| to order | to tell s.o. to do s.th. | befehlen |
| angrily | "Stop talking, Class 6!" said the teacher *angrily*. | zornig |
| servant | s.o. who works in another person's house | Diener |
| earl | aristocrat in England | Graf |
| to break in | Chris broke in while I was speaking (*to break, broke, broken*) | *h:* unterbrechen |
| of course | naturally; *Of course* I'll help you! | natürlich |
| still | I can't come out – I'm *still* doing my homework. | (immer) noch |
| to call | The Sheriff *calls* Prince John "Sire". | *h:* nennen |
| to go on | Stop talking and *go on* with your work. | fortfahren; *h:* weiterreden |
| to marry | Samuel wants to *marry* my sister. | heiraten |
| tomorrow | It's Sunday today, so *tomorrow* will be Monday. | morgen |
| feast | wonderful meal | Festmahl; Festessen |
| slowly | *opp.* quickly | langsam |
| in front of | *opp.* behind | vor (*räumlich*) |
| enemy | *opp.* friend | Feind |
| even | This book is so easy that *even* I can read it. | sogar; auch |
| true | *opp.* false | wahr |
| fool | stupid person | Narr; Dummkopf |
| to shout | He *shouted* for help. *opp.* to whisper | schreien |
| to need | This plant is yellow – it *needs* water. | brauchen; benötigen |
| quietly | He spoke so *quietly* that I couldn't hear him. | leise |
| later | I'm working now – can we talk *later*? | später |
| church | Some people go to *church* every Sunday. | Kirche |
| everything | *opp.* nothing | alles |
| ready | Breakfast is *ready* – come and eat! | bereit |
| wedding | when a man and a woman marry | Hochzeit |

| | | |
|---|---|---|
| guest | person who comes to a party, wedding *etc.* | Gast |
| place | Barbara! Go to your *place* and sit down! | *h:* (Sitz-)Platz |

**PAGE 5**

| | | |
|---|---|---|
| bride | woman on her wedding-day | Braut |
| together | Cathy and Jenny always walk to school *together.* | zusammen |
| dressed | For the party, Max was *dressed* in his best T-shirt. | gekleidet |
| colour | Blue, green and red are *colours.* | Farbe |
| leaf (*pl.* leaves) | *Leaves* are green things on flowers and trees. | Blatt |
| each | *Each* boy and girl in the class has a chair. | jeder (einzelne) |
| to carry | The mother *carried* the baby to bed. *(to wear, wore, worn = Kleider tragen!)* | *(in Armen, Händen)* tragen |
| longbow | *old word for* bow | (Lang-)Bogen |
| abbot | chief man in a monastery *(= Kloster)* | Abt |
| already | I ran to the bus stop, but the bus had *already* left. | schon |
| tall | Sally is one metre sixty *tall.* | groß; hochgewachsen |
| knight | Have you heard of King Arthur's *knights*? | Ritter |
| everyone | all the people | jedermann |
| to turn round | She *turned round* to look at the boy behind her. | s. (um-)drehen |
| smile | happy look on your face; *verb:* to smile | Lächeln |
| to follow | Saturday *follows* Friday. | folgen |
| proudly | "This is a wonderful class!" the teacher said *proudly.* | stolz |
| until | She will stay in the class *until* summer. | bis |
| greenwood | *old word for* forest *or* wood | Wald; tiefer Wald |
| to promise | My parents have *promised* to take me to London. | versprechen |
| safe | Will the baby be *safe*, alone? | sicher; in Sicherheit |
| face | Have you washed your *face*? | Gesicht |
| sword | long knife for fighting | Schwert |
| spear | long stick with a metal point *(= Spitze)* | Speer |
| arrow | This is what you shoot from a bow. | Pfeil |
| bowstring | the part of the bow that you pull and then let go | Bogensehne |
| to thrust | to push s.th. hard (*to thrust, thrust, thrust*) | stossen |
| heart | When I run, my *heart* beats fast. | Herz |
| to step | to move your feet | schreiten; treten |
| the flat | *h:* not the part that cuts! | *h:* die flache Seite |
| own | These books are the school's, but this is my *own.* | eigen |
| helmet | Firemen wear *helmets.* | Helm |
| ground | An apple fell to the *ground.* | Boden |
| stunned | If you're *stunned*, you can't see, think or talk for a while. | benommen |
| without | You can't buy things *without* money! *opp.* with | ohne |
| leader | chief person | (An-)Führer |
| cheer | the shout 'Hurray!' or 'Hurrah!' | Freudenruf; Hurra |
| woods | forest | Wald |
| soon | I worked fast and *soon* finished my homework. | bald |
| to disappear | The train *disappeared* into the tunnel. *opp.* to appear | verschwinden |
| among | The teacher stands *among* the girls and boys. | (mitten) unter; inmitten |

**PAGE 7**

| | | |
|---|---|---|
| secret | No one knows this – it is *secret.* | geheim; verborgen |

| | | |
|---|---|---|
| path | The *path* led through the garden to the house. | Pfad; Weg |
| to reach | Phone me when you *reach* London! | erreichen |
| wide | *opp.* narrow | breit |
| clearing | place in the forest with no trees | Lichtung |
| oak | kind of tree | Eiche |
| cave | Thousands of years ago people lived in *caves*. | Höhle |
| deep | The water is so *deep* – it's over my head! | tief |
| dry | Wood will burn if it's *dry*. *Opp.* wet | trocken |
| belt | thing that you wear round your waist (= *Taille*) | Gürtel |
| to roast | to cook *(meat)* in an oven or on a fire | braten; rösten |
| piece | Would you like a *piece* of cake? | Stück |
| venison | meat from a deer | Wildbret; Rehfleisch |
| enormous | very big; An elephant is an *enormous* animal. | riesig |
| dark | At night it is *dark*. *Opp.* light | dunkel |
| no one | *No one* is with me – I am alone. *Opp.* everyone | niemand; keiner |
| to be afraid of | *Are* you *afraid of* rats? (*to be, was/were, been*) | Angst haben vor |
| cruel | The *cruel* boy was hitting the little dog. | grausam; hart |
| to hurt | Helen *hurt* her leg when she fell. (*to hurt, hurt, hurt*) | verletzen; wehtun |
| to fear | Sometimes, little children *fear* the dark. | fürchten |

**CHAPTER 2 – HOW LITTLE JOHN JOINED THE OUTLAW BAND**

| | | |
|---|---|---|
| to happen | The accident (= *Unfall*) *happened* at 3 o'clock. | geschehen; passieren |
| always | Why do you *always* get up so late? *Opp.* never | immer |
| to travel | He often *travels* by train. | reisen |
| food | We need *food* and drink to live. | Essen; Nahrung |
| to want (to) | The little boy cried because he *wanted to* go home. | wollen |
| to have to | I *had to* do my homework before I could go out. | müssen |
| alone | After his wife died, he lived *alone*. | alleine |
| to listen | If you *listen* to the teacher, you will learn better. | zuhören |
| river | The Amazon and the Nile are both big *rivers*. | Fluss |
| wet | If you fall into the water, you will get *wet*. | nass |
| to lie | Toby *lay* on the bed reading a book. (*to lie, lay, lain*) | liegen |
| bank | We got out of the boat onto the *bank*. | Ufer |
| bridge | s.th. built over a river *etc.* to let us go over it | Brücke |
| however | I have no computer. I could, *however*, buy one. | jedoch; aber |
| to notice | to see | bemerken; beobachten |
| to move | Don't *move*, or I will shoot! | s. bewegen |
| the same | His birthday is *the same* as mine. *Opp.* different | der/die/dasselbe; der/die/das gleiche |

**PAGE 8**

| | | |
|---|---|---|
| soon | I worked fast and *soon* finished my homework. | bald |
| both | *both* men = the two men | beide |
| tree trunk | the thick part of a tree | Baumstamm |
| to cross | to go from one side to the other | überqueren |
| to wait (for) | We *waited* at the bus-stop until the bus came. | warten (auf) |
| in a flash | very quickly | im Nu |
| coward | person who is afraid of everything | Feigling |
| quarterstaff | long stick for fighting with | Bauernspiess; Schlagstock |
| giant | very big man | Riese; Hüne |

| | | |
|---|---|---|
| blow | In the fight, he got such a *blow* that he fell down. | Schlag |
| to push | Help! Someone *pushed* me into the water! | stossen; schieben |
| heavy | I can't carry this bag – it's too *heavy*. *Opp.* light | schwer (*Gewicht*) |
| to swish | Robin's arrow *swished* through the air. | zischen; sausen |
| after a while | after a time | nach einiger Zeit |
| to breathe | We can't *breathe* under water. | atmen |
| at last | in the end; after some time | schließlich |
| head-first | He is in hospital – he fell *head-first* down the stairs. | kopfüber |
| to pull | The little girl was crying, "Billy *pulled* my hair!" | ziehen; zerren (an) |
| together | Cathy and Jenny always walk to school *together*. | zusammen |

**PAGE 10**

| | | |
|---|---|---|
| certainly | of course; naturally | gewiss; sicher(lich) |
| to join | Ken has *joined* the tennis club. | *h:* Mitglied werden |
| seriously | not playing or making a joke | ernst(-haft) |
| to roar | to make a loud noise | brüllen |
| tear | Look! He's crying! His eyes are full of *tears*. | Träne |
| life | Have you lived in England all your *life*? | Leben |
| idea | Some more homework? – No! That's a bad *idea*! | Idee; Gedanke |

**CHAPTER 3 – HOW ROBIN HOOD WON THE SILVER ARROW**

| | | |
|---|---|---|
| month | January, February and March are *months*. | Monat |
| archery | shooting a bow | Bogenschießen |
| contest | game that people try to win | Wettkampf; Wettbewerb |
| prize | what you give to s.o. who has won a contest | Preis (*den man gewinnt*) |
| magnificent | The king has a *magnificent* palace. | herrlich |
| feather | Birds are covered with *feathers*. | (Vogel-)Feder |
| dinner | hot meal eaten in the evening | (warmes) Abendessen |
| archer | person who shoots a bow | Bogenschütze |
| country | Germany is a *country* in Europe. | Land |
| everybody | The school is empty – *everybody* has gone home. | jedermann; alle |
| to watch | to look at (s.o. or s.th.) for some time | zuschauen |
| in disguise | in different clothes, to change how you look | verkleidet |
| nobody | The school is empty – *nobody* is here. *Opp.* everybody | niemand |
| dangerous | Broken glass is *dangerous*. | gefährlich |
| nonsense | It's *nonsense* to say that eggs grow on trees. | Unsinn |
| firmly | Teachers must speak *firmly* to this class. | entschlossen; bestimmt |
| of course | naturally; *Of course* I'll help you. | natürlich |
| That's that! | That is the end of that! | Damit basta! |
| brightly | with a lot of light | hell |
| far and wide | People came from *far and wide* to see our class play. | weit und breit |
| to take part | *to take part* in a game = to be one of the players | teilnehmen |
| to mark out | The field was *marked out* for a game of football. | abgrenzen; markieren |
| royal | the *Royal* Family = the king, queen *etc.* | königlich; Königs- |
| stand | Here, people can stand or sit to watch sports. | Tribüne |
| applause | There was loud *applause* when our team won. | Beifall |
| excellent | Sarah – your English test was *excellent*! | hervorragend; ausgezeichnet |

**PAGE 11**

| | | |
|---|---|---|
| only | That class is very small – it has *only* ten children. | nur |
| to be left | He has spent all his money – there *is* nothing *left*. | übrig bleiben; übrig sein |

| | | |
|---|---|---|
| forester | s.o. who works in a forest | Förster |
| Delamere | *former forest in North-West England* | früheres Waldgebiet im Nordwesten Englands |
| Wirral | *area near Chester, in North-West England* | Gebiet in Nordwestengland |
| hood | this goes over your head | Kapuze |
| herald | person who carries messages from a king | Herold |
| target | what Robin Hood shoots at with his arrows | Ziel(-scheibe) |
| to fire | to shoot | schießen |
| to take a deep breath | If you want to swim underwater, you must *take a deep breath* first. (*to take, took, taken*) | tief durchatmen |
| to aim | to point a bow, gun *etc.* at s.th. or s.o. | zielen |
| crowd | There was a big *crowd* at the concert. | (Menschen-)Menge |
| to murmur | to say s.th. very quietly | murmeln; raunen |
| to hiss | The snake *hissed*. | zischen |
| roar | *h:* shouting and applause | *h:* tobender Beifall |
| to paint | Picasso *painted* that picture. | malen |
| spot | A tiger has stripes and a leopard has *spots*. | Fleck; Tupfen |

**PAGE 12**

| | | |
|---|---|---|
| thumbnail | hard part at the end of your thumb (= *Daumen*) | Daumennagel |
| close | near | nah |
| quiet | still; *opp.* loud | still; ruhig |
| to clap | The parents *clapped* when the children had finished. | klatschen |
| excitedly | "It's my first time in a plane!" he said *excitedly*. | aufgeregt |
| cheer | "You can have longer holidays!" she said, and there were *cheers* from the class. | Jubelruf |
| It was his turn. | I read my work first, and then *it was* Julian*'s turn*. | Er war an der Reihe. |
| hard-faced | a *hard-faced* man = a man with a hard face | mit harter Miene |
| to whisper | She *whispered* so that she wouldn't wake the baby. | flüstern |
| to work | His plan was no good – it didn't *work*. | *h:* „klappen"; funktionieren |
| to raise | to lift | heben |
| hardly | She speaks so quietly that I can *hardly* hear her. | kaum |
| to dance | *h:* to jump up and down because you are so happy | *h:* vor Freude hüpfen |
| sharply | "Forgotten, Jerry? Again?" said the teacher *sharply*. | scharf |
| to ask | He *asked* me, "Can you speak English?" | fragen |
| reply | answer | Antwort |
| perhaps | *Perhaps* I'll see him tomorrow, but I don't know. | vielleicht |
| traitor | person who hurts his friends, his country *etc.* | Verräter |
| For shame! | You should be ashamed! | Pfui!; Schämen Sie sich! |
| strange | What is that *strange* noise in the corridor? | seltsam; merkwürdig |
| to pass | to go by (s.o. or s.th.) | vorbeigehen; vorbeikommen |
| in a flash | very quickly | im Nu |
| to disappear | The train *disappeared* into the tunnel. | verschwinden |
| Excuse me! | Forgive me! | Entschuldigen Sie! |

**PAGE 13**

| | | |
|---|---|---|
| almost | Two minutes to eight! It's *almost* time for school! | fast; beinahe |
| past | We couldn't get on the bus because it drove *past*. | vorbei |

**PAGE 14**

| | | |
|---|---|---|
| air | this comes into our lungs when we breathe (= *atmen*) | Luft |

| | | |
|---|---|---|
| at least | That book will cost *at least* £20. | mindestens; wenigstens |
| low | She has such a *low* voice that I can't hear her. | *h:* leise; schwach |
| groan | "No homework today!" The class gave a *groan*. | Stöhnen |
| to escape | to get away; to get free | entkommen |
| figure | *h:* person | Gestalt |
| robes | long, loose clothes | Gewänder |
| wide | This is too *wide* – I can't jump over it. | breit |
| to jump | If you shoot at a horse, it will *jump*. | *h:* scheuen (*Pferd*) |
| saddle | seat for a rider on a horse | Sattel |
| mud | After the football match, he was covered in *mud*. | Schlamm; Dreck |
| surprise | She got a *surprise* when she heard the news. | Überraschung |
| to frighten | Don't shout – you'll *frighten* the baby. | erschrecken |
| to pick up | The mother *picked up* the crying baby. | (auf-)heben; (hoch-)heben |
| to carry | I *carried* my friend's schoolbag to the bus. | (*in Armen, Händen*) tragen |
| slim | nicely thin; *opp.* plump | schlank |
| no idea | What's 'school' in Chinese? I've *no idea*! | keine Ahnung |
| to scratch | The little boy cried when the cat *scratched* him. | kratzen |
| to wonder | I don't know that boy – I *wonder* who he is. | s. fragen |
| who on earth | *Who on earth* wants more homework? | wer in aller Welt |

**CHAPTER 4 – THE COMING OF FRIAR TUCK**

| | | |
|---|---|---|
| friar | a sort of priest | Bruder (*Mönch*) |
| autumn | *Autumn* comes between summer and winter. | Herbst |
| whose | That is the boy *whose* leg was broken. | dessen; deren |
| except for | *Except for* Sunday, he works every day. | außer; abgesehen von |

**PAGE 15**

| | | |
|---|---|---|
| to remember | *opp.* to forget | s. erinnern an |
| to knock | I *knocked* the glass off the table and it broke. | schlagen; stoßen |
| to beat | I can *beat* my father at tennis. (*to beat, beat, beaten*) | besiegen; schlagen |
| eagerly | "Please let me go in your boat!" she said *eagerly*. | eifrig |
| monk | sort of priest | Mönch |
| across | Don't walk *across* the road if a car is coming. | (quer) über |
| surely | You are so clever – *surely* you know the answer! | sicher(lich); gewiss |
| edge | He fell off the *edge* of the cliff. | Rand |
| shield | Robin's arrows hit the fat man's *shield*. | Schild |
| to lie | Toby *lay* on the bed reading a book. (*to lie, lay, lain*) | liegen |
| ground | We sat on the *ground* to eat our picnic. | Boden; Erde |
| nearby | Let's go and see Emily – she lives *nearby*. | in der Nähe |
| to whistle | Chris *whistled* happily as he worked. | pfeifen |
| cheerfully | happily | fröhlich; munter |
| otherwise | Walk slowly on the ice, *otherwise* you'll fall. | sonst |
| to get up | The little boy *got up* onto his father's back. (*to get, got, got*) | *h:* aufsteigen |
| even | I am good at English, but my brother is *even* better. | *h:* noch |
| heavy | I can't carry this bag – it's too *heavy*. *Opp.* light | schwer (*Gewicht*) |
| to pant | He ran all the way to school and sat there *panting*. | keuchen |

**PAGE 16**

| | | |
|---|---|---|
| patiently | The old man waited *patiently* at the bus stop. | geduldig |
| to bother | Don't *bother* me with silly questions! | belästigen; stören |

| | | |
|---|---|---|
| quite | It's *quite* warm today. | ganz |
| wrong | It is *wrong* to say that 2 + 2 = 5. | falsch |
| real | This is *real* gold, not just yellow metal. | echt; wirklich |
| to ring | *h:* to echo (*to ring, rang, rung*) | *h:* wiederhallen |
| sound | what you can hear | Klang |
| to thrust | She *thrust* the money into my hand and ran away. (*to thrust, thrust, thrust*) | stoßen |
| hour | 60 minutes | Stunde |
| certainly | of course; naturally | gewiss; sicher(lich) |
| to burst | The balloon *burst* when I sat on it. (*to burst, burst, burst*) | platzen; bersten |
| only | That class is very small – it has *only* ten children. | nur |
| a few | Can I have *a few* flowers for the table? | ein paar |
| What's the matter? | What's wrong? What's the problem? | Was ist los? |
| priest | *Priests* have to work on Sundays. | Priester |
| like | Sally has a pullover *like* mine. | wie |
| stomach | The children were lying flat on their *stomachs*. | *h:* Bauch |
| worried | My mother will be *worried* if I come home late. | besorgt; beunruhigt |
| to shine | Jenny is very happy – her eyes are *shining*. (*to shine, shone, shone*) | *h:* leuchten; strahlen |

**PAGE 18**

| | | |
|---|---|---|
| to sigh | The teacher *sighed* when I forgot my homework. | seufzen |
| terrible | School on Sundays? That's *terrible*! | schrecklich |
| nothing but | Some people eat *nothing but* fast food. | nichts als |
| ale | kind of English beer | (*englisches*) Bier |
| day after day | every day; all the time | Tag für Tag |
| barrel | big thing for holding beer or wine | Fass |
| to beam | Frances *beamed* when she won the prize. | (*vor Freude*) strahlen |
| indeed | Helen is a good rider. – Yes, *indeed* she is! | in der Tat; tatsächlich |
| against | I am *against* your plan. | gegen |
| to add | "And stop eating chewing-gum!" he *added*. | hinzufügen |
| bottom | When you sit down, your *bottom* is on the chair. | *h:* Hintern; ‚Popo' |

**CHAPTER 5 – ROBIN HOOD AND THE BISHOP**

| | | |
|---|---|---|
| bishop | important (= *wichtig*) priest | Bischof |
| so | The shop is closed, *so* you can't buy any bread. | deshalb |
| really | What do you *really* want for your birthday? | wirklich |
| place | A school is a *place* where people work and learn. | Ort |
| including | I know all his family, *including* the baby. | einschließlich |
| shepherd | A *shepherd* is a person who looks after sheep. | Hirte |
| beside | next to | neben |
| track | small path or road | Weg |
| to light | Please *light* the fire. | anzünden |
| delicious | Mmm – this ice-cream is *delicious*! | köstlich |
| smell | A *smell* of cooking came from the kitchen. | Geruch |
| rider | person on a horse | Reiter |
| nervously | "Must I go there alone?" he asked *nervously*. | nervös |
| signal | Normally, a red light is a *signal* to stop. | Zeichen |

| | | |
|---|---|---|
| to smell | That fish smells bad. (*to smell, smelt, smelt*) | riechen |
| meat | Hamburgers are made of *meat.* | Fleisch |
| mercy | The King had *mercy* on the rebels. | Erbarmen; Gnade |
| to feed | The mother *feeds* her baby with a spoon. (*to feed, fed, fed*) | ernähren; füttern |
| to moan | The class *moaned* about the English test. | jammern; stöhnen |
| to pardon | to forgive | vergeben |

**PAGE 20**

| | | |
|---|---|---|
| shocked | I was *shocked* when I saw what he had done. | entrüstet; empört |
| to tremble | She *trembled* when I shouted at her. | zittern |
| dinner | warm meal in the evening | (warmes) Abendessen |
| to pay for s.th. | If you want these shoes, you must *pay for* them. (*to pay, paid, paid*) | etwas bezahlen |
| during | *During* the day, the sun gives us light. | während |
| miserably | The little girl was crying *miserably.* | elend; totunglücklich |
| finally | After a long time, we *finally* found the lost child. | schließlich |
| to finish | Have you *finished* your homework? | beenden |
| unwilling | I asked him to come, but he was *unwilling.* | unwillig |
| guest | How many *guests* came to your party? | Gast |
| little | I am tired – I slept very *little* last night. | wenig |
| Never mind! | Don't worry about it! | Machen Sie sich nichts draus! |
| to mutter | We *mutter* when we have too much homework. | *h:* murren |
| enough | There is *enough* chocolate for everyone. | genug |
| saddle-bag | bag behind a saddle on a horse's back | Satteltasche |
| coin | piece of money | Münze |
| Coins rained down. | Coins fell down like rain. | Es regnete Münzen. |
| purse | small bag where you keep money | Geldbeutel |
| bag | She came home with a shopping *bag* full of food. | Beutel; Tasche |
| boot | high, heavy shoe ; He wore some old army *boots.* | Stiefel |
| to count | My little sister can *count* from 1 to 10. | zählen |
| friendly | The new teacher gave me a *friendly* smile. | freundlich |
| comfort | s.th. that makes you feel better | Trost |

**PAGE 21**

| | | |
|---|---|---|
| voice | With my *voice,* I can speak and sing. | Stimme |
| to believe | I couldn't *believe* my eyes when I saw her blue hair! | glauben; *h:* trauen |
| to clap | We *clapped* when our class won the prize. | klatschen |
| to trot | to ride slowly | traben |
| to stare | to look for a long time | starren |
| tail | Cats, cows, mice and elephants all have *tails.* | Schwanz |
| tightly | The little boy held his mother's hand *tightly.* | fest |

**CHAPTER 6 – HOW ROBIN HOOD MET THE SHERIFF**

| | | |
|---|---|---|
| to be surprised | I *was surprised* that my English test was so good. | überrascht sein |
| cart | wagon pulled by horses | Wagen |
| fresh | These eggs came *fresh* from the farm today. | frisch |
| next to | My best friend sits *next to* me in class. | neben |
| apron | thing that you wear to keep your clothes clean | Schürze |

| | | |
|---|---|---|
| butcher | person who sells meat | Metzger |
| politely | "Thank you very much!" they said *politely.* | höflich |
| nice | Let's go out – it's a *nice* day for a walk. | nett; schön |
| to sell | *opp.* to buy (*to sell, sold, sold*) | verkaufen |
| market | Every Saturday is *market* day in our town. | Markt |
| to lend | Can you *lend* me a pencil? I've forgotten mine. | leihen |
| as well | Kathy is learning English, and Latin *as well.* | dazu; außerdem |
| to put on | *Put on* your coat – it's very cold outside. | anziehen |
| rather | When I had finished work, I was *rather* tired. | ziemlich; *h:* etwas |
| pound | Could I have a *pound* of apples, please? | Pfund |

**PAGE 23**

| | | |
|---|---|---|
| for sale | We are leaving town, so our house is *for sale.* | zu verkaufen |
| to finger | Don't *finger* those cakes! | betasten |
| pocket | He stood there with his hands in his *pockets.* | Tasche (*Hose, Kleid* ...) |
| housewife | wife or mother who looks after a home | Hausfrau |
| to crowd | to all come together | s. drängen; s. scharen |
| cheap | *opp.* expensive | billig |
| to take no notice | *Take no notice* of him = Don't listen to him / don't look at him. | nicht darauf achten |
| wife | *opp.* husband | (Ehe-)Frau |
| both ... and ... | Lisa speaks *both* French *and* English. | sowohl ... als auch |
| by now | Where is he? He should be here *by now.* | *h:* inzwischen |
| good-looking | All the boys in this class are very *good-looking*! | gut aussehend |
| delight | The wonderful class was a *delight* to the teacher. | Freude |
| to learn | From the letter, I *learnt* that Rita was ill. | *h:* erfahren |
| prisoner | person who has been caught and is not free | Gefangene(r) |
| cattle | cows, bulls and oxen | Vieh |
| to set off | We must *set off* early in the morning. | aufbrechen |
| at first | at the beginning | zuerst |
| profit | If you buy a book for £10 and sell it for £15, you have made a *profit* of £5. | Gewinn; Profit |
| further | Judith walked two kilometres *further* than Ann. | weiter |
| quiet | Be *quiet* – the baby is asleep. | still |
| quite | He is *quite* good at English, but I am better. | ganz |
| eagerly | "Please let me go in your boat!" she said *eagerly.* | eifrig |
| hiding-place | where you go so that no one can find you | Versteck |
| bend | curve | Kurve |
| proudly | "This is a wonderful class!" the teacher said *proudly.* | stolz |
| to lick | The dog *licked* its master's hand. | lecken |

**PAGE 24**

| | | |
|---|---|---|
| to blindfold | to cover (*s.o.'s eyes*) so that he can't see | die Augen verbinden |
| although | *Although* I am tired, I can't stop working. | obwohl |
| to notice | to see | merken; bemerken |
| afterwards | later | nachher |
| to come to | The new books *came to* £60. | *h:* s. belaufen auf |
| to spend | Larry has *spent* all his money – he has none left. | ausgeben |
| to stay | My sister went out, but I *stayed* at home. | bleiben; verbleiben |
| to spit | The baby *spat* its food on the floor. | spucken |

| | | |
|---|---|---|
| whenever | Come and see me *whenever* you like. | wann auch immer |

**CHAPTER 7 – THE RETURN OF THE KING**

| | | |
|---|---|---|
| return | coming back | Rückkehr |
| ballad | kind of song | Ballade; Volkslied |
| careful | Be *careful* – there's ice on the road! | vorsichtig |
| fork | At the *fork*, you must take the road on the left. | *h:* Gabelung |
| to part | She waved goodbye when we *parted*. | s. trennen |
| path | This *path* goes from the road to our house. | Pfad; Weg |
| stranger | s.o. that you don't know | Fremde(r) |

**PAGE 25**

| | | |
|---|---|---|
| to show | to let s.o. see s.th. | zeigen |
| stump | When you cut a tree down, this stays in the ground. | (Baum-)Stumpf |
| to point | "Who is that?" he asked, *pointing* at the new boy. | hindeuten |
| to sneer | They *sneered* at him because his family was poor. | spötteln |
| target | Robin's arrows always hit the *target*. | Ziel(-scheibe) |
| knife | thing for cutting or fighting | Messer |
| heart | When I run, my *heart* beats fast. | Herz |
| coward | person who is afraid of everything | Feigling |
| instead | I don't like potatoes. Could I have rice *instead*? | stattdessen |
| to flash | to go by very quickly | *h:* flitzen; fliegen |
| to thud | to make a low, heavy sound | dumpf (auf-)schlagen |
| to miss | *opp.* to hit | *h:* nicht treffen |
| both | the two | beide |
| to draw | *h:* to pull out | ziehen |
| men on horseback | men riding horses | berittene Männer |
| to tie | to bind | binden |
| news | Have you heard the *news*? The Queen is coming! | Nachricht(en) |
| to reward | I'm going to *reward* the person who finds my dog. | belohnen |
| excited | I was *excited* when I saw that our class was winning. | aufgeregt |
| rope | They tied the boat to the tree with a long *rope*. | Seil; Schnur |
| to whisper | She *whispered* so that she would not wake the baby. | flüstern |

**PAGE 26**

| | | |
|---|---|---|
| a fight to remember | "A thing *to remember*" is a thing that you will never forget. | ein Kampf, den niemand vergessen würde |
| again | Say it *again* – he didn't hear you. | wieder; nochmal |
| difficult | *opp.* easy | schwierig |
| to climb | The boy *climbed* up the tree. | klettern; steigen |
| dressed as | in the clothes of | gekleidet als |
| pilgrim | Many *pilgrims* go to Rome or Jerusalem. | Pilger |
| the Holy Land | Israel | das Heilige Land |
| oak | sort of tree | Eiche |
| to beg for | She *begged* me *for* money, but I said no. | betteln um; bitten um |
| He waved his hand. | I asked him to take me to the cinema, but *he* just *waved his hand*. | *h:* Er winkte ab. |
| later | I can't talk to you now – ask me *later*. | später |
| to enjoy oneself | The children all *enjoyed themselves* at the party. | s. amüsieren |

| | | |
|---|---|---|
| usually | normally; We *usually* go to church on Sundays. | gewöhnlich; normalerweise |
| buffets | *old word which means* blows | Schläge |
| in return | Lend me your bike, and you can borrow my radio *in return*. | dafür; zurück |
| fist | Boxers hit each other with their *fists*. | Faust |
| to strike | to hit; He *struck* me with a stick. | schlagen |
| to raise | to lift up | heben |
| to knock | to hit | schlagen |
| to clap | We *clapped* when our class won the prize. | klatschen |

**PAGE 28**

| | | |
|---|---|---|
| huge | very big | riesig |
| to gasp | He was *gasping* when I pulled him out of the water. | keuchen |
| honour | good name; respect | Ehre |
| to shake | The cat took the rat in its mouth and *shook* it. | schütteln |
| flat | '*Flat* on the ground' is the opposite of 'upright.' | flach |
| to smile | Julian *smiled* because he was happy to see us. | lächeln |
| wide | *opp.* narrow | breit |
| real | This is *real* gold, not just yellow metal. | echt; wirklich |
| gesture | Shaking your head is a *gesture*. | Geste |
| to ask | The poor man *asked* me to give him some money. | bitten |
| to need | We *need* water to live. | brauchen; benötigen |
| important | The President is an *important* person. | wichtig |
| each other | Ann and Judy write letters to *each other*. | einander |
| at the head | Your name is *at the head* of the list. | *h:* an der Spitze |
| to welcome | Mr Thomas *welcomed* us to his house. | willkommen heißen |
| to flee | to run away | fliehen |

# Exercises

*The following exercises offer over 800 questions, ranging from "Yes, he did"-forms over grammar, vocabulary and comprehension to question-forming, short talks and suggestions for written retellings: in all, a wide variety which the teacher can choose from to suit the needs of different classes.*

- ✧ *If pupils are not used to this kind of material, it is important to introduce the different exercise types orally in class, letting pupils gain experience before doing questions as homework.*
- ✧ *In class, pupils can work all together, individually or in small groups of two to four. The work can be done spontaneously in class, prepared in class or prepared at home. Homework can be written out normally for the teacher or prepared in draft form for oral work in class.*
- ✧ *The class could divide themselves and an exercise into three parts and do, for example, questions 1–3, questions 4–6 and questions 7–9. Preparation time is thus reduced, but pupils are still exposed to the full range of material through the others' contributions. Different groups of the class can work on different exercises, and assignments can be rotated for the following homework or practice sessions.*
- ✧ *When all the main types of exercise have been worked on, some groups may enjoy this: Each child chooses (freely, or with guidance) an exercise from the repertoire of those already worked on. This must be so prepared that answers can be given orally without looking at the text or printed exercise. The questions can be asked – in or out of order – by the class and/or teacher.*

✧ *One useful vocabulary exercise is not included here, because it can be played* extempore. *The teacher (or a pupil) reads out parts of the text that have been worked on, missing out, because of alleged hiccoughs, suitable words – which must then be supplied by the class. Instead of the gap in speaking (for the hiccough), a traditional variant is to use the code, 'teapot', for the word to be guessed. If this variant is played, then 'teapot' must be inflected etc. if needed. Thus: "Everywhere there were* Teapots, *full of fat deer" and "John was* teapotting *a great feast in the Sheriff's castle."*

**Exercise 1 – Who** (page 3) **INTRODUCTION**

1. Who was King of England?
2. Who was Robin Hood?
3. Who had left England to fight in the Holy Land?
4. Who was Prince John?
5. Who had John driven into the forest as outlaws?
6. Who suffered even more?
7. Who grew fat, while the king's friends lived as outlaws?
8. Who had been made a prisoner on his way back from the Holy Land?

**Exercise 2 – What** (page 3)

1. What was much wilder, in those days?
2. What was full of deer belonging to the king?
3. What did Prince John love?
4. What did he take from many rich men?
5. What did a penniless father often kill, to feed his children?
6. What would John's men do, if they caught a man killing a deer?
7. What did the friends of King Richard hope?
8. What did Prince John say when he heard that his brother was a prisoner?

**Exercise 3 – Who** (page 4) **CHAPTER 1**

1. Who was drinking wine in the hall of the castle?
2. Who stood at all the doors?
3. Who were the two men?
4. Who was happy that Prince John would soon be king?
5. Who was the man who came running in?
6. Who plans to marry Lady Marian Fitzwalter?
7. Who kills the deer in the king's forests?
8. Who needs Sir Guy of Gisborne's help?

**Exercise 4 – Either/Or** (page 4)

1. Were the two men standing at the doors or drinking wine?
2. Was Prince John talking with the Sheriff or with his brother, King Richard?
3. Did the man walk into the hall with the soldiers, or did he come running in?
4. Did the Sheriff jump up, or did he fall on his knees?
5. Was the man Robert Fitzooth, or was he a servant?

6. Does Earl Robert live in Nottingham or at Locksley?
7. Does he plan to get married in two days' time, or the next evening?
8. Will he hold a great feast in two days' time, or the next evening?

**Exercise 5 – Word Order** (page 4)

*Put the word or expression in italics into the sentence given. If it could go in several places, then show all the correct positions you can find.*

1. Two men were drinking wine. *(in Nottingham Castle)*
2. A man came running into the hall. *(suddenly)*
3. The Sheriff jumped up. *(looking angrily at the guards)*
4. Prince John took away Earl Robert's lands. *(last year)*
5. The people call Earl Robert their lord. *(still)*
6. Earl Robert has a house at Locksley. *(still)*
7. He plans to get married. *(in two days' time)*
8. He is going to hold a great feast. *(tomorrow evening)*

**Exercise 6 – Who and Where** (pages 4–5)

1. Where was everything ready for Robert Fitzooth's wedding?
2. Who were in their places?
3. Who was there with the bride?
4. Where was Earl Robert, when the men in green came in?
5. Who came into the church suddenly?
6. Where did the fat abbot run?
7. Who followed him?
8. Where will Earl Robert live now?

**Exercise 7 – Short Answers** (pages 4–5)

1. Was everything ready for the wedding?
2. Were the guests in their places?
3. Was Earl Robert together with the bride?
4. Were the men who came in dressed in Lincoln green?
5. Was the abbot waiting to begin?
6. Was Earl Robert fat?
7. Were horses heard outside the church?
8. Was the tall knight Lady Marian's father?

**Exercise 8 – Put into the Past Tense** (pages 4–5)

1. Suddenly, horses *are* heard outside.
2. A tall knight *enters* the church.
3. Everyone *turns* to look at him.
4. The fat abbot *runs* out of the church.
5. Many of the guests *follow* him.
6. Marian *wants* to be Earl Robert's wife.

7. Earl Robert *speaks* proudly to the knight.
8. Then he *walks* out of the church.

**Exercise 9 – Mixed Questions** (page 5)

1. What was hard?
2. What did the soldiers hold in their hands?
3. Who did the soldiers see in front of them?
4. Where did Guy thrust his sword?
5. What did Robin hit with the flat of his sword?
6. Who turned to run?
7. Where did Robin's men run to?
8. When did Sir Guy see only the sun shining on the forest?

**Exercise 10 – Let Earl Robert Tell the Story!** (page 5)

*Rewrite these sentences as if you were Earl Robert. For example:*
***Earl Robert** held a feast at **his** house. ⇨ **I** held a feast at **my** house.*

1. Robert saw Sir Guy's soldiers with their spears.
2. He looked at his men.
3. Guy thrust his sword at Robert's heart.
4. Earl Robert stepped to one side.
5. He swung the flat of his sword to hit Guy's helmet.
6. Then he shouted to his men to follow him.
7. Robert's men gave a cheer and ran into the woods with him.
8. Sir Guy couldn't see Earl Robert or his men.

**Exercise 11 – Describing a Picture** (page 6)

1. Make at least five sentences about the picture on page 6.
   You can begin: *"In the picture I can see ..."*

**Exercise 12 –What, Where and When** (page 7)

1. What did Robin's men run along?
2. What did they reach, deep in the greenwood?
3. Where were the caves?
4. Where did Robin take his horn from?
5. Who came out of the caves to meet them?
6. Where did the outlaws roast great pieces of venison?
7. When did Robin Hood stand up and speak to his men?
8. Where did the men kneel down and give their promise?

**Exercise 13 – Asking Questions** (pages 4–7)

*"Ask your teacher ..." can, of course, refer to anyone else who may be suitable!*
*Ask your teacher ...*

1. ... if two men were drinking in the castle.
2. ... if one of the men was Prince John.

3. ... if the Sheriff of Nottingham was happy that John would be king.
4. ... if Robert Fitzooth was the Earl of Huntingdon.
5. ... if the wedding guests were in their places.
6. ... if Lincoln green was the colour of the leaves of the forest.
7. ... if Sir Guy was stunned when Earl Robert hit him.
8. ... if the caves were in a wide clearing.

**Exercise 14 – Vocabulary** (pages 4–7)

1. What do we call *a place where thousands of trees grow?*
2. What is the opposite of *a friend*?
3. What is the opposite of *to whisper?*
4. What is the opposite of *loudly?*
5. What is the word for *a place where we go to pray to God?*
6. What is the name for *a person that you ask to come to a party or a wedding?*
7. What word means *with other people* (the opposite of *alone*)?
8. What is the opposite of a *short* person, a *short* tree?
9. What word means *all the people* (the opposite of *no one*)?
10. What is the opposite of *with?*
11. What is the word for *a place in the forest where there are no trees?*
12. What is a word meaning *very, very big?*

**Exercise 15 – Did You Understand the Chapter?** (pages 4–7)

1. Why was Prince John happy?
2. What surprised the two men while they were talking?
3. What news did the servant bring?
4. Why did Prince John already know about Robin Hood?
5. What was Sir Guy ordered to do at the church?
6. Why did the abbot and many of the guests run away?
7. What was the bride's answer to Robin's question?
8. How did the fight outside the church begin?
9. How did Robin end it?
10. What promise did the men in the forest give?

**Exercise 16 – Retelling the Story** (pages 4–7)

*Talk about one of the following topics to the class, in just a few sentences. Write things down if you like, but when you speak to the class the rule is: no notes, no pieces of paper and no text! If you're nervous, give your notes to the teacher, who can be your 'prompter'. The numbers after each topic show you where to look: 5,22 means page 5, line 22.*

1. Prince John, the Sheriff and the Servant (4,1–4,29)
2. In the Church (4,30–5,23)
3. Robin and Sir Guy (5,24–5,35)
4. In the Forest (7,1–7,17)

**Exercise 17 –Who, What and Where** (pages 7–8)

1. Who did Robin Hood meet one day?
2. Where would Robin often wander alone?
3. What did he come to, walking through the forest one morning in summer?
4. Where had one of the trees fallen?
5. Who did he notice on the other bank?
6. What did Robin think?
7. Who soon reached the bridge?
8. Where did each man have his foot?

**Exercise 18 – Short Answers** (pages 7–8)

1. Did Robin Hood have many fine fighting men?
2. Did he always want to hear what was happening?
3. Would he often wander through the forest alone?
4. Would his men come to help him if he blew his horn?
5. Was he walking through the forest one morning?
6. Was it one morning in winter?
7. Did he see someone on the other bank?
8. Did the big man swim across the river?

**Exercise 19 – Put into the Past Tense** (pages 7–8)

1. Robin *is* walking through the forest one morning.
2. He *comes* to a small river.
3. Robin *does* not want to get his feet wet.
4. He *sees* that one of the trees *has* fallen directly across the river. *(Two verbs!)*
5. But as he *walks* towards it, he *notices* someone on the other bank. *(Two verbs!)*
6. It *is* the biggest man he *has* ever seen. *(Two verbs!)*
7. Soon both men *come* to the bridge.
8. They *stand* there, one on each side of the river.

**Exercise 20 – Either/Or** (page 8)

1. Did Robin have a sword or a bow and arrow?
2. Did the big man have a quarterstaff or a spear?
3. Is a quarterstaff a stick or a sword?
4. Did Robin put his bow over his shoulder or on the ground?
5. Was the tree that Robin cut as tall as he was, or much shorter?
6. Did the two men fight in the water or on the tree trunk?
7. Did they fight with their fists or with heavy sticks?
8. Who fell into the river – Robin or the giant?

**Exercise 21 – Asking Questions** (page 8)

*Ask your teacher ...*

1. ... if Robin had a bow and arrow in his hands.

2. ... what Robin had in his hands.
3. ... if the big man shouted at Robin.
4. ... what the big man shouted at Robin.
5. ... if Robin wanted to cut himself a staff.
6. ... where Robin wanted to cut himself a staff.
7. ... if the heavy sticks swished through the air.
8. ... when the heavy sticks swished through the air.

**Exercise 22– What Really Happened?** (page 8)

*The person who wrote these sentences has got everything wrong.*
*Can you tell the story as it really was?*

1. "After you, Giant!" said Robin. "You can cross the bridge first!"
2. "Oh, no, sir!" the giant said. "I will wait till you've crossed!"
3. Robin fell to his knees and said, "Please come over the bridge before me!"
4. "You wonderful person!" said the big man. He smiled at Robin.
5. Slowly, Robin climbed up a tree in the forest.
6. Soon, the two men were sitting together on the tree trunk.
7. Then they began singing a long English song.
8. At last, the giant jumped into the river for a little swim.

**Exercise 23 –Describing a Picture** (page 9)

1. Make at least five sentences about the picture on page 9.
   You can begin: *"In the picture I can see ..."*

**Exercise 24 – Mixed Questions** (pages 8–10)

1. Who pulled the big man into the river?
2. Where did the two men sit after the fight?
3. What did Robin take now?
4. Where was the big man going when he met Robin?
5. Who came running out of the trees?
6. What was the big man's real name?
7. Who roared with laughter?
8. What did Much, the miller's son have in his eyes?

**Exercise 25 – Vocabulary** (pages 7–10)

1. What is the opposite of *never?*
2. What word means *things that we can eat?*
3. With our eyes, we can see and look. With our ears, we can hear and ......
4. Water is ...... (the opposite of *dry*).
5. What is the opposite of *different?*
6. What is one word for *in a short time?*
7. What is the word for *to go from one side to the other?*
8. What is the opposite of *light* in a *light* schoolbag?

9. What do we call *the front of our head, where our eyes, nose and mouth are?*
10. What is the opposite of *alone?*
11. What is one word meaning *Yes, of course, naturally?*
12. What do we call *a drop of water in someone's eye, from crying or laughing?*

**Exercise 26 – Making Sentences** (pages 7–10)

*Make up at least one sentence for each of the following words or expressions. You can stay close to the text or invent your own: not too long, but also not too short. The sentences can be as serious or amusing as you like, but not embarrassing!*

1. One day ...
2. ... always wanted to ...
3. Wait – I'll ...
4. I hope you ...
5. Suddenly, he took ...
6. ... looked at ...
7. Perhaps ...
8. ... a good idea ...

**Exercise 27 –Did You Understand the Chapter?** (pages 7–10)

1. Why did Robin often wander through the forest alone?
2. Why did he have the big horn at his belt?
3. Why didn't Robin just walk through the river?
4. Why did Robin start walking more quickly?
5. Who reached the bridge first?
6. Why did Robin put his bow on the ground?
7. What was Robin's staff like?
8. Why did Robin fall into the water?
9. How did the two men feel after the fight?
10. Why did the outlaws all laugh at John Little's name?

**Exercise 28 – Retelling the Story** (pages 7–10)

*See the instructions for Exercise 16. Do at least one topic as written work!*
*The starred (*) topic is more ambitious, and covers the material of the whole chapter.*

1. How the Meeting Happened (7,26–8,4)
2. The Fight (8,5–8,26)
3. After the Fight (8,27–10,13)
4. * How Little John Joined the Outlaws (7,18–10,13)

**Exercise 29 – Who** (page 10) **CHAPTER 3**

1. Who was going to hold an archery contest?
2. Who spoke to his men that evening?
3. Who must go to the contest in Nottingham?
4. Who is the best archer in the country?

5. Who would love to catch Robin?
6. Who will go to Nottingham with Robin?
7. Who sat in the royal stand?
8. Who stood on the other side of the piece of land?

**Exercise 30 – Short Answers** (page 10)

1. Were Prince John and the Sheriff going to hold an archery contest?
2. Would the prize be magnificent?
3. Did Robin speak to his men after dinner that evening?
4. Is Will Scarlett the best archer in the country?
5. Will Robin go to Nottingham in disguise?
6. Will his men let him go to Nottingham alone?
7. Did the people of Nottingham sit with Prince John and his friends?
8. Was the shooting excellent?

**Exercise 31 – Who, What and Where** (pages 11–12)

1. Who was left in the contest, by mid-afternoon?
2. Where will the targets be set now?
3. Who was the first of the three men to shoot?
4. Where would the heralds paint the 'eye' – the small white spot?
5. What did the Sherwood man wear on his head?
6. What did the hard-faced man whisper to Prince John?
7. Where did the Sherwood man's arrow hit the target?
8. What did the people of Nottingham do then?

**Exercise 32 – Either/Or** (pages 11–12)

1. How many archers were left by mid-afternoon – two, three or four?
2. Who wore a brown hood – the man from Delamere, or the Sherwood man?
3. Will each man have two shots, or only one?
4. Who hit the gold now – all three men, or only the Sherwood man?
5. Were the people very quiet while the archers were shooting, or did they shout and clap?
6. Who was the hard-faced man in the royal stand – Prince John or Sir Guy?
7. Was the crowd happy or sad that the Sherwood man had won?
8. Did they stand there silently, or did they cheer and dance?

**Exercise 33 – Describing a Picture** (page 11)

1. Make at least five sentences about the picture on page 11.

**Exercise 34 –Put into the Future Tense** (pages 11–12)

1. The heralds *set* the targets at two hundred yards.
2. The man from Delamere *shoots* first.
3. Now the Wirral man *takes* a deep breath and *fires*.
4. The Sherwood man's arrow *hits* the gold too.

5. A roar *goes* up from the crowd.
6. Prince John *watches* the man from Sherwood very closely.
7. Guy of Gisborne *whispers* in Prince John's ear.
8. The man from Sherwood *wins* the prize.

**Exercise 35 – Who and What** (page 12)

1. What was hidden by the Sherwood man's brown hood?
2. Who told the man to take off his hood?
3. Who pulled the hood back?
4. What did Prince John give the man from Sherwood?
5. What were this man's two names?
6. What did Prince John say to the guards?
7. Who whispered something in Prince John's ear?
8. What did Prince John say to the soldiers after this?
9. Who disappeared among the crowd?
10. Who was waiting for the outlaw?

**Exercise 36 –Put into the Past Tense** (page 12)

1. The Sherwood man *kneels* before Prince John.
2. His face *is* hidden by his brown hood.
3. A soldier *pulls* back the hood.
4. Prince John *stands* up slowly.
5. He *asks* the man what his name *is*. *(Two verbs!)*
6. Sir Guy *knows* that the man *is* Robin Hood. *(Two verbs!)*
7. He *whispers* something in Prince John's ear.
8. Prince John *gives* a strange smile.

**Exercise 37 – Short Answers** (pages 13–14)

1. Did Robin leave the field now?
2. Did six of his men join him?
3. Was the contest a plan to catch Robin?
4. Will Sir Guy's soldiers be waiting for the outlaws?
5. Did the outlaws go directly towards the trees?
6. Did they see soldiers coming towards them?
7. Did Robin begin to run?
8. Could they see about twenty soldiers in front of them now?
9. Was Guy of Gisborne riding a white horse?
10. Was he in the middle of the soldiers?
11. Did Robin see Little John with an arrow in his leg?

**Exercise 38 – Word Order** (pages 13–14)

*See the instructions for Exercise 5.*

1. The outlaws saw a group of trees. *(in front of them)*

2. They moved through the fields. *(silently)*
3. A strange figure in brown sprang out of the trees. *(suddenly)*
4. Sir Guy shouted, "Kill him!" *(angrily)*
5. A second figure was seen. *(as he shouted) (in the trees)*
6. Sir Guy fell. *(out of the saddle) (backwards)*
7. He landed. *(by the river) (heavily) (in the mud)*
8. Robin shouted. *(almost) (with surprise)*

**Exercise 39 – Describing a Picture** (page 13)

1. Make at least five sentences about the picture on page 13.

**Exercise 40 – Asking Questions** (pages 13–14)

*Ask your teacher ...*

1. ... if the outlaws moved silently.
2. ... how the outlaws moved.
3. ... if they heard a shout.
4. ... when they heard a shout.
5. ... if they saw more soldiers in front of them.
6. ... where they saw more soldiers.
7. ... if the archer in the trees was Lady Marian.
8. ... who the archer in the trees was.

**Exercise 41 – What Really Happened?** (pages 13–14)

*See the instructions for Exercise 22.*

1. "Prince John will be waiting for us alone," said Robin.
2. Behind them, they saw a secret path.
3. The outlaws stamped loudly through the trees.
4. Suddenly, they heard Prince John laughing.
5. Robin and his men lay down on the grass.
6. The forest was miles away, and they saw nobody.
7. In the field was a white pony with the Sheriff on its back.
8. Out of the trees near the Sheriff came Little John with a bow.
9. *Swish!* The pony jumped, and the Sheriff sprang into the river.
10. Robin almost began to cry. Little John had frightened the pony!

**Exercise 42 – Making Sentences** (pages 10–14)

*See the instructions for Exercise 26.*

1. News came to ...... that ...
2. ... would love to ...
3. only
4. He hardly seemed to ...
5. ... looked at ...
6. Perhaps ...

7. Suddenly, ...
8. ... shouted angrily ...

**Exercise 43 – Vocabulary** (pages 10–14)

1. January, April, August and October are the names of .........
2. What is the name for *a hot meal eaten in the evening?*
3. What is the word for *extremely good* or *very, very good?*
4. What do we call *a big group of people, all standing together?*
5. What is the word for *to shout 'Hurrah! Hurrah!'?*
6. What is the opposite of *to shout?*
7. What is another word for *to answer?*
8. What is another word for *maybe* or *it is possible that?*
9. What is a word meaning *to run away so that people can't catch you?*
10. This is the word for *earth and water, mixed together.*

**Exercise 44 – Did You Understand the Chapter?** (pages 10–14)

1. What were Prince John and the Sheriff planning now?
2. What was Robin's reaction?
3. What problem did Will Scarlett see?
4. What did the heralds decide when all three men hit the gold *(page 11)*?
5. What was Guy of Gisborne's plan?
6. Why were the people of Nottingham so happy?
7. Why did Prince John let Robin go?
8. Why did the outlaws go silently around the trees?
9. Why did Sir Guy fall off his horse?
10. Why did Robin almost shout with surprise?

**Exercise 45 – Retelling the Story** (pages 10–14)

*See the instructions for Exercise 16. Do at least one topic as written work!*

1. Going to Nottingham (10,14–10,31)
2. An Exciting Contest (11,1–12,16)
3. Before Prince John (12,16–12,33)
4. How the Outlaws Escaped (13,1–14,19)

**Exercise 46 – Who and What** (pages 14–15) **CHAPTER 4**

1. What did the outlaws hold contests in?
2. Who was the only one who could shoot a deer from 250 yards?
3. Who is the best fighter in England, in Robin's opinion?
4. Who does Little John think is the best fighter?
5. Who might beat both Robin and Little John?
6. What would you think when you saw this friar?
7. What was the man, before the abbot threw him out?
8. What does he do now?

**Exercise 47 – Put into the Present Tense** (pages 14–15)

*Be careful of the sentences with more than one verb!*

1. It *was* autumn now in Sherwood, and life *was* good.
2. The outlaws *held* contests in archery.
3. Little John *was* the only one who *could* hit a deer at 250 yards.
4. Then Will Scarlett *told* them about a big fat friar.
5. This man *lived* on the other side of the forest.
6. He *liked* fighting very much.
7. He *carried* people over the river on his back.
8. He *was* called Friar Tuck.

**Exercise 48 – Short Answers** (pages 15–16)

1. Did Robin reach a wide river?
2. Could he see a bridge?
3. Was the monk almost as tall as Robin?
4. Did Robin want to cross the river?
5. Did he want to carry the friar on his back?
6. Was the fat friar even heavier than he looked?
7. Did Robin throw the friar into the river?
8. Was Robin now back where he started?

**Exercise 49 – Either/Or** (pages 15–16)

1. Was the monk much shorter than Robin, or almost as tall?
2. Was he wearing a sword at his side, or just a small knife?
3. Did Robin give the man money, or did he put his hand on his sword?
4. Did the monk say nothing, or did he shout at Robin?
5. Did Robin want to go swimming, or did the monk throw him into the water?
6. When Robin got out of the water, did he take his bow first or his sword?
7. Did he want to kill the man with his arrows or just frighten him?
8. Did the fat friar catch the arrows with his shield, or did he run away?

**Exercise 50 – Asking Questions** (pages 15–16)

*Ask your teacher ...*

1. ... if the friar wanted to be on the other side of the river.
2. ... where the friar wanted to be.
3. ... if Robin almost fell while he was carrying the friar.
4. ... why Robin almost fell.
5. ... if the friar threw Robin into the cold water.
6. ... when the friar threw Robin into the cold water.
7. ... if Robin shot twelve arrows at the fat man.
8. ... how many arrows Robin shot at the fat man.
9. ... if a real fight began now.

**Exercise 51 – Put into the Past Tense** (page 16)

1. The friar *turns* patiently and Robin *gets* up on his back.
2. Robin *wonders* if he *is* bothering the wrong person.
3. But in the middle of the river, the friar *throws* him into the water.
4. Robin *is* wet from head to foot and *fires* an arrow to frighten the monk.
5. But the man *swings* his shield and *catches* the arrow.
6. At last, Robin *springs* into the water and *crosses* over.
7. The river bank *rings* with the clash of swords, but the friar *does* not move back.
8. After an hour, Robin's sword *feels* heavy in his hand.

**Exercise 52 – Let Robin Answer the Questions!** (page 16)

*Answer these questions as if Robin himself were speaking.*
*Use the Past Tense, as in the questions.*
*For example: Where **did you go**? ⇨ **I went** to Nottingham.*

1. Where did you put your hand when you looked into the man's eyes?
2. What did you do when the friar turned patiently?
3. What did the friar do in the middle of the river?
4. What did you take when you reached the other bank?
5. How did you aim your first arrow?
6. How many arrows did you shoot?
7. What did you do when you had fired all your arrows?
8. How did the fight go on now?

**Exercise 53 – Describing a Picture** (page 17)

*So far, you've probably made short sentences, like: "I can see Little John" or "I can see Robin's bow". For this exercise, you should make longer sentences. Instead of just naming a person or thing, try to make up three different parts after the "I can see ..."*

| | | | | |
|---|---|---|---|---|
| *Examples:* | *I can see* | *①Guy's soldiers* | *②stand**ing*** | *③outside the church.* |
| | *I can see* | *①Robin* | *②fight**ing*** | *③Little John.* |
| | *I can see* | *①Sir Guy* | *②fall**ing*** | *③off his horse.* |

1. What can you see in the picture on page 17?
   Write several longer sentences.

**Exercise 54 – Who and Where** (pages 16–18)

1. Who blew his horn ?
2. Where did the two men lie down?
3. Where did the men in green come running from?
4. Who called to Robin?
5. Where would it be good to have a priest like Friar Tuck?
6. Where did the friar put his hand?
7. Who threw back his head and laughed?
8. Who hurt his bottom, falling off his horse?
9. Where did the outlaws go, laughing?

**Exercise 55 – What Really Happened?** (page 15–16)

*See the instructions for Exercise 22.*

1. The monk was much smaller than Robin, and very thin.
2. He had a bow in his hand, and there was a sword on the ground nearby.
3. "Take me across the river in your boat, please," said Robin.
4. Robin was standing on the bank of the river when he fell in.
5. The friar swam through the water to help him.
6. The Sheriff's men fired arrows at Robin.
7. Robin began to fight the Sheriff's men with a long stick.
8. Robin said that the friar was too fat, and should not come to Sherwood.

**Exercise 56 – Making Sentences** (pages 14–18)

*See the instructions for Exercise 26.*

1. ... the only one who ...
2. I remember how ...
3. I'd like to ...
4. I don't want to ...
5. Robin wondered if ...
6. After an hour, ...
7. What do you ... ?
8. ... nothing but ...

**Exercise 57 – Vocabulary** (pages 14–18)

1. What is the opposite of *to forget*?
2. What is the word for *land at the side of a river*?
3. What is the opposite of *light* (as in a *light* shield)?
4. What is the opposite of *far away*?
5. What is another word for *happily*?
6. What is the opposite of *dry*?
7. What is the opposite of *last*?
8. What is the opposite of *right* (as in the *right* person)?
9. What is a word meaning *to make someone afraid?*
10. What is the opposite of *at the edge*?
11. What is a word meaning *60 minutes*?
12. What do we do when we hear a good joke?

**Exercise 58 – Did You Understand the Chapter?** (pages 14–18)

1. How did the outlaws spend their time that autumn?
2. Why was Robin so eager to meet the friar?
3. Why did the friar now live alone?
4. What did the monk look like?
5. Why did Robin put his hand on his sword?
6. Did Robin fall into the water by accident?

7. What was the one thing the friar was worried about?
8. Why did the friar help the outlaws against Sir Guy's men?

**Exercise 59 – Retelling the Story** (pages 15–18)

*See the instructions for Exercise 16. Do at least one topic as written work!*

1. Robin Wants to Cross the River (15,15–15,24)
2. Into the River (15,25–16,6)
3. The Fight (16,7–16,18)
4. After the Fight (16,19–18,4)

**CHAPTER 5**

**Exercise 60 – Who and Where** (page 18)

1. Where would the Bishop of Hereford soon be passing?
2. Where did most of the outlaws hide?
3. Who put on shepherds' clothes?
4. Where was the bishop, in the group of riders?
5. Where were the soldiers?
6. Who smelt the meat and broke off?
7. Who will hang the shepherds?
8. Who got off their horses?

**Exercise 61 – Short Answers** (page 18)

1. Did Robin hear that Prince John would be passing through the forest?
2. Was the Bishop of Hereford one of the richest men in England?
3. Did most of the men hide in the trees?
4. Did all the men put on shepherds' clothes?
5. Was the bishop riding a fine white horse?
6. Did he smell the meat?
7. Did the shepherds look very frightened?
8. Did the bishop get off his horse?

**Exercise 62 – Put into the Past Tense** (page 18)

1. Robin *hears* about the Bishop of Hereford.
2. The bishop *is* one of the richest men in England.
3. So Robin really *wants* to meet him.
4. Most of the outlaws *hide* among the trees and *wait*.
5. But some of them *sit* down and *light* a fire.
6. Then they *begin* to roast a great piece of venison.
7. When the bishop *sees* them, he *gives* the signal to stop.
8. Then he *smells* the meat and *breaks* off.

**Exercise 63 – Describing a Picture** (page 19)

*See the instructions for Exercise 53.*

1. What can you see in the picture on page 19?
   Write several longer sentences.

**Exercise 64 – Word Order** (pages 18–20)

*See the instructions for Exercise 5.*

1. Robin wanted to meet the bishop. (*really*)
2. The outlaws lit a fire. (*beside the track*)
3. There was a delicious smell of roasting meat. (*all around*) (*soon*)
4. The soldiers looked around them. (*nervously*)
5. The bishop spoke to the shepherds. (*loudly*)
6. The soldiers left the bishop with outlaws around him. (*alone*)
7. The outlaws will give the bishop dinner. (*here in Sherwood*)
8. They went along the secret paths of the forest. (*off*)

**Exercise 65 – Put into the Present Tense** (page 20)

1. The shepherd *took* a horn from his belt and *blew* it.
2. Soon the trees *were* full of men in Lincoln green.
3. The soldiers *jumped* onto their horses and *galloped* off.
4. They *left* the bishop alone with the outlaws.
5. They *went* along the secret paths, while the bishop *trembled.*
6. He *was* too frightened to see where they *were* going.
7. The outlaws *laughed* and *drank* at the feast.
8. But the bishop *sat* miserably till the meal *was* finished.

**Exercise 66 – What Really Happened?** (pages 18–20)

*See the instructions for Exercise 22.*

1. Robin Hood was one of the richest men in England.
2. Prince John was a friend of Robin's.
3. Some shepherds put on the bishop's clothes.
4. They warmed their shoes on a fire, and soon there was a terrible smell.
5. Now a group of outlaws came running into the clearing.
6. To the left and right of the bishop, monks walked slowly.
7. In seconds, the trees were full of foresters in brown hoods.
8. They had big sticks in their hands, and began to fight the outlaws.

**Exercise 67 – Mixed Questions** (page 20)

1. When did Robin turn to his unwilling guest?
2. Who was this unwilling guest?
3. What didn't the guest like?
4. What rained down onto the grass?
5. Where did the bishop have bags of money?
6. Where did he have the small bags?
7. How much money did the bishop have?
8. Who was cheerful?

**Exercise 68 – Either/Or** (pages 20–21)

1. Did the bishop laugh and drink, or did he sit miserably?
2. Did Robin turn to his guest before the meal, or after it?
3. Must the bishop pay for his meal, or is it free?
4. Has he got fine meat in his saddle-bags, or golden coins?
5. Are there bags of gold under his shirt, or under his hat?
6. Will all this gold buy things for the outlaws, or will it help poor people?
7. Must the bishop sing for the outlaws, or must he do a dance?
8. Did the bishop have an excellent voice, or was it not very good?

**Exercise 69 – Let the Bishop Tell the Story!** (pages 18–21)

*Tell the story as if you were the Bishop of Hereford. Leave the verb forms in the Past Tense.*
*For example: **The bishop** rode into the forest. ⇨ **I** rode into the forest.*

1. The bishop rode into Sherwood Forest.
2. He had his soldiers beside him.
3. When he saw the shepherds, he gave his men the signal to stop.
4. He smelt the meat, and the shepherds begged him for mercy.
5. When the outlaws came, the bishop's men galloped off and left him there.
6. He was so frightened he couldn't see where the outlaws were taking him.
7. After the meal, Robin Hood's men took all his gold.
8. They made him sing, too, but his voice was not very good.

**Exercise 70 – Asking Questions** (pages 18–21)

*Ask your teacher ...*

1. ... if most of the men hid among the trees.
2. ... where most of the men hid.
3. ... if the bishop gave the signal to stop.
4. ... what signal the bishop gave.
5. ... if the outlaws will give the bishop dinner.
6. ... what they will give him.
7. ... if the bishop began to sing.
8. ... what kind of song he began to sing.

**Exercise 71 – Vocabulary** (pages 18–21)

1. What is the opposite of *poor*?
2. What do we call *a person who looks after sheep*?
3. With my eyes, I can see. With my nose, I can ......
4. What do we call *the men who fight in an army*?
5. What is the opposite of *quietly*?
6. If you haven't eaten for a long time, you must be ......
7. What is the word for *to give money for something*?
8. What is a word for *very unhappily*?

9. What does the bishop have on his feet? Not *shoes*, but ......!
10. What is another word for *at last*?

**Exercise 72 – Did You Understand the Chapter?** (pages 18–21)

1. Why did Robin want to meet the bishop?
2. Why did some outlaws put on shepherds' clothes?
3. Why did the bishop's soldiers look nervously around them?
4. Who was the 'shepherd' who talked with the bishop?
5. Why did Robin say, "No pardon for you, Lord Bishop!"?
6. What did Robin want to do with the bishop's money?
7. Why did the outlaws want to hear the bishop sing?
8. How did they send him back to Nottingham?

**Exercise 73 – Retelling the Story** (pages 18–21)

*See the instructions for Exercise 16. Do at least one topic as written work!*

1. Meeting the Bishop (18,11–20,1)
2. The Outlaws Come Out (20,2–20,16)
3. The Feast (20,17–20,35)
4. Afterwards (21,1–21,13)

**CHAPTER 6**

**Exercise 74 – What and Where** (page 21)

1. What did Robin hear in the forest one day?
2. Where did the short man walk?
3. Where was the butcher hoping to sell his meat?
4. What did Robin have now?
5. What did the butcher lend Robin?
6. Where did the butcher lie down to sleep?
7. What did Robin put on?
8. Where did the old horse walk off towards?

**Exercise 75 – Put into the Past Tense** (page 21)

1. One day in the forest, Robin hears someone whistling.
2. Out of the trees come a horse and cart.
3. A short man walks next to the cart.
4. He is whistling loudly, but he stops when he sees Robin.
5. He trembles and then stares at Robin.
6. Robin has a sudden idea, and asks to buy the man's meat.
7. The butcher thinks that this is a wonderful idea.
8. So Robin puts on the man's clothes and goes off towards Nottingham.

**Exercise 76 – Describing a Picture** (page 22)

*See the instructions for Exercise 53.*

1. What can you see in the picture on page 22?
   Write several longer sentences.

**Exercise 77 – Who** (page 23)

1. Who were soon crowding around Robin's cart?
2. Who stared at Robin?
3. Who took no notice of people calling to him?
4. Who looked at the meat and bought several pounds?
5. Who would be at dinner with Robin and the Sheriff's wife?
6. Who was a prisoner in Europe?
7. Who wanted to be king himself?
8. Who wanted to know if his guest had cattle to sell?

**Exercise 78 – Either/Or** (page 23)

1. Was a penny a pound for meat expensive, or was it cheap?
2. Who crowded around Robin's cart – housewives, or the other butchers?
3. Was the Sheriff's wife alone, or was the Sheriff with her?
4. Did she just look at the meat, or did she buy some?
5. Did Robin talk to the Sheriff's wife, or did he talk to the other butchers?
6. Did the Sheriff's wife ask Robin to help her or to come to dinner?
7. Was dinner at the castle or at the Sheriff's house?
8. Did the Sheriff want to buy cattle or to sell them?

**Exercise 79 – Put into the Future Tense** (page 23)

1. The next morning, Robin and the Sheriff *set* off together.
2. Only two men *go* with them.
3. At first, the Sheriff *is* cheerful, but soon he *grows* quieter.
4. In the forest, his eyes *look* nervously to left and right.
5. Then the men *come* round a bend in the track.
6. They *see* a great herd of deer, and Robin *says*, "Look – my cattle!"
7. The Sheriff *licks* his lips nervously, and Robin *blows* his horn.
8. A lot of outlaws *come* out of the bushes. They *grin* at the Sheriff.

**Exercise 80 – What and When** (page 23)

1. When did Robin and the Sheriff set off together?
2. What was the Sheriff thinking of, at first?
3. When did he grow quieter?
4. What would the Sheriff pay well to see?
5. When did Robin and the Sheriff see the herd of deer?
6. What did Robin call the deer?
7. When did the outlaws come out of the bushes?
8. What did they do when they saw the Sheriff?

**Exercise 81 – Short Answers** (page 24)

1. Was the Sheriff right to be nervous?
2. Will the Sheriff pay to see Robin Hood's hiding-place?

3. Were the Sheriff and his men blindfolded?
4. Did the outlaws give them a fine feast?
5. Did the Sheriff eat a lot of food?
6. Did the Sheriff's gold come to five hundred pounds?
7. Could the three prisoners reach town from the Nottingham road?
8. Would their horses stay in the forest?

**Exercise 82 – Asking Questions** (page 24)

*Ask your teacher ...*

1. ... if the Sheriff was led to the great clearing.
2. ... if he had little appetite.
3. ... if the outlaws counted the Sheriff's gold.
4. ... what they counted.
5. ... if it came to five hundred pounds.
6. ... how much it came to.
7. ... if the outlaws laughed loudly.
8. ... why the three prisoners were blindfolded again.

**Exercise 83 – Making Sentences** (pages 21–24)

*See the instructions for Exercise 26. You can change the words in italics, if you want.*

1. ... was/were surprised to ...
2. ... was/were hoping to ...
3. ... is/are much too ...
4. By now, *Robin* had already ...
5. ... asked *him* to ...
6. At first ..., but then ...
7. ... was/were planning to ...
8. ... can/could easily ...

**Exercise 84 – Let the Sheriff Answer the Questions!** (pages 23–24)

*Answer these questions with 'Short Answers' as if the Sheriff himself were speaking. As usual, you should leave the tenses as they are in the questions.*

*For example: **Are you** the Sheriff of Nottingham? ⇨ Yes, **I am**.*

1. Do you want to buy any cattle?
2. Will you come with me tomorrow?
3. Will you bring a lot of soldiers with you?
4. Did you set off with the butcher the next morning?
5. Were you thinking of the profit you would make?
6. Would you pay well to see Robin Hood's hiding place?
7. Did you and your men see deer in the forest?
8. Were you and your men blindfolded?
9. Could you see the way to the outlaws' secret place?
10. Are you Robin Hood's friend?

**Exercise 85 – Vocabulary** (pages 21–24)

1. I was ...... when the teacher said today was a holiday.
2. What do we call *a person who works with meat*?
3. What is the word for *to give something to a person for money*?
4. What is the opposite of *to be awake*?
5. What is the opposite of *expensive*?
6. Morning, afternoon, ......, night.
7. What is the opposite of *no one*?
8. This word means *the day after today*.
9. What word means *with a cloth round your eyes so that you can't see*?

**Exercise 86 – Did You Understand the Chapter?** (pages 21–24)

1. Why did the butcher look nervously at Robin?
2. Why did Robin want to borrow the butcher's clothes, and his cart?
3. Why did Robin sell his meat for only a penny a pound?
4. Why was Robin happy to go to the Sheriff's house for dinner?
5. What did the Sheriff tell Robin about King Richard?
6. Why did the Sheriff want to buy cattle?
7. Why didn't the Sheriff eat much at the feast?
8. Why did he and his men have to walk home?

**Exercise 87 – Retelling the Story** (pages 21–24)

*See the instructions for Exercise 16. Do at least one topic as written work!*

1. Meeting the Butcher (21,14–21,28)
2. Nottingham (21,29–23,19)
3. Into the Forest (23,20–24,2)
4. The Sheriff's Gold (24,3–24,17)

**Exercise 88 – Special Retelling** (Introduction and Chapters 1–5)

*In this exercise, you will be asked to retell what you can remember from earlier chapters. Some topics you can probably talk about without looking back at the text. If you do re-read a page, then don't spend longer than five minutes or so looking at it.*

1. England at the Time of Robin Hood (page 3)
2. In Nottingham Castle (page 4)
3. Outside the Church (page 5)
4. After the Fight on the Bridge (pages 8–10)
5. Escape from Nottingham (pages 13–14)
6. Crossing the River Three Times (pages 15–16)
7. How Robin Took the Bishop into the Forest (pages 18–20)

**Exercise 89 – Who** (page 24) **CHAPTER 7**

1. Who sang ballads about Robin's men?
2. Who did the outlaws rob?
3. Who did they help?

4. Who did the outlaws hope would return?
5. Who was planning something?
6. Who were very careful?
7. Who was Robin walking through the forest with, one day?
8. Who did he notice, among the trees?

**Exercise 90 – Put into the Past Tense** (page 25)

1. Robin *points* at a tree stump, but the stranger *sneers*.
2. So Robin *puts* down his bow and *cuts* a branch with his knife.
3. Now he *hears* the man's voice again, and *knows* it well.
4. Sir Guy *stands* in front of him, and his bow *is* aimed at Robin's heart.
5. Robin *throws* his knife at Sir Guy.
6. It *flashes* past Guy's ear, and Guy's arrow *misses* Robin.
7. The two men *draw* their swords, and the fight *begins*.
8. It *doesn't* last long: soon Sir Guy *lies* dead on the ground.

**Exercise 91 – Asking Questions** (pages 24–25)

*Ask your teacher ...*

1. ... if people sang ballads about the men of Sherwood.
2. ... what people sang.
3. ... if Robin soon noticed a figure among the trees.
4. ... where Robin soon noticed a figure.
5. ... if the stranger's friends would laugh at such an easy target.
6. ... what his friends would laugh at.
7. ... if the fight lasted long.
8. ... how long the fight lasted.

**Exercise 92 – What** (page 25)

1. What did Robin hear, very soon?
2. What was suddenly full of men on horseback?
3. What had the Sheriff's men heard?
4. What did 'Sir Guy' point to?
5. What did the Sheriff want to give 'Sir Guy'?
6. What did 'Sir Guy' ask for, instead?
7. What did Robin have in his hand?
8. What did he cut through?

**Exercise 93 – Short Answers** (page 26)

1. Did Robin give a loud laugh?
2. Was the fight a fight to remember?
3. Did the outlaws fight well?
4. Had the Sheriff brought an army with him?
5. Did Robin's men fight with their bows?

6. Did Robin blow his horn?
7. Was the Sheriff surprised to see the knight in black armour?
8. Did his men want a difficult fight?

**Exercise 94 – Put into the Future Tense** (pages 25–26)

1. Soon the clearing *is* full of men on horseback.
2. The Sheriff *brings* six of Robin's men with him.
3. The prisoners' hands *are* tied behind their backs.
4. Robin *speaks* to the Sheriff in Sir Guy's voice.
5. Then he *moves* behind the outlaws. With his knife, he *cuts* their ropes.
6. A great fight *begins*, and the outlaws *take* swords from the soldiers.
7. Robin *blows* his horn, and a knight in black *rides* into the clearing.
8. He *helps* the outlaws, and the Sheriff's men *gallop* back to Nottingham.

**Exercise 95 – Mixed Questions** (page 26)

1. When did Robin meet a new figure in the forest?
2. How was the man dressed?
3. Where did Robin keep his hand?
4. Where did the outlaws eat a great feast?
5. Who seemed to like his food?
6. What did the men beg for, afterwards?
7. How do the outlaws play *buffets*?
8. When do they usually play *buffets*?

**Exercise 96 – Either/Or** (page 26)

1. Did Robin meet the new figure that afternoon or a few days later?
2. Was the man dressed as a knight or as a pilgrim?
3. Were all the outlaws friends of the King, or only a few of them?
4. Did the pilgrim like his food, or did he have little appetite?
5. Did the outlaws want news of the Holy Land, or news of King Richard?
6. Did the man tell them his news, or did he say, "Later! Later!"?
7. Did they play a game after the meal, or did they sing songs?
8. Was *buffets* real fighting, or were the outlaws only playing?

**Exercise 97 – Let the Pilgrim Tell the Story!** (pages 26–28)

*Tell the story as if you were the pilgrim. Leave the verbs in the Past Tense. For example:*
***The pilgrim*** *met Robin Hood in the forest.* ⇨ ***I*** *met Robin Hood in the forest.*

1. Much, the miller's son struck the pilgrim hard.
2. The pilgrim raised his arm and knocked Much down.
3. Will and Little John buffeted him, but his fist struck them like a hammer.
4. Then he sent Friar Tuck flying off his feet.
5. At last, Robin's arm swung, and the stranger almost fell.
6. He shook his head slowly, and then raised his own arm.

7. Robin fell down on his back under the stranger's blow.
8. The pilgrim smiled down at him.

**Exercise 98 – Describing a Picture** (page 27)

*See the instructions on making longer sentences for Exercise 53.*

1. What can you see in the picture on page 27?
   Write several longer sentences.

**Exercise 99 – Who** (pages 26–28)

1. Who struck the first blow, in the game of *buffets*?
2. Who shouted and clapped when Will Scarlett stood up?
3. Who whistled in surprise when he fell?
4. Who was the third man to hit the pilgrim?
5. Who was the outlaws' only hope?
6. Who fell flat on his back by the fire?
7. Who did he see smiling down at him?
8. Who was the pilgrim?

**Exercise 100 – Put into the Present Tense** (page 28)

1. Robin's arm *swung*, and the stranger almost *fell*.
2. The stranger *shook* his head slowly, and then *raised* his own arm.
3. Robin *opened* his eyes and *saw* his friends looking at him.
4. He *was* lying flat on his back by the fire.
5. The pilgrim *smiled* and *pulled* back his hood.
6. The outlaws *saw* that it *was* the King, and *fell* on their knees.
7. King Richard *made* a gesture for them to sit down again.
8. The King *wanted* to find out who his real friends *were*.

**Exercise 101 – Making Sentences** (pages 24–28)

*See the instructions for Exercise 26.*

1. No one knew where/when/what ...
2. ... noticed ...
3. ... again.
4. If you like, then ...
5. Suddenly, ...
6. ... well
7. ... didn't want ...
8. ... have been ... for ...

**Exercise 102 – Vocabulary** (pages 24–28)

1. What is the word for *twelve months*?
2. What is another word for *to come back*?
3. What do we call *a thing that you shoot at*?
4. What do we use to cut things with?
5. What is the opposite of *alive*?

6. The Sheriff's men tied the outlaws' hands with ......
7. What is the word for *a place in the forest where there are no trees*?
8. What is a word meaning *to go after* someone?
9. What is the opposite of *difficult*?
10. What is a word meaning *to say* something *very loudly*?
11. What is the opposite of *weak*?
12. What is another word for *to go away*, or *to go away from*?
13. What do we call *the time when a man and woman get married*?

**Exercise 103 – Did You Understand the Chapter?** (pages 24–28)

1. Why were the outlaws very careful?
3. How did the stranger make Robin put down his bow?
4. How did Robin stop Sir Guy from killing him?
5. Was the Sheriff a good fighter?
6. Why did Robin keep his hand on his sword when he met the pilgrim?
7. What happened during the game of *buffets*?
8. Why did King Richard come first as a knight, and then as a pilgrim?
9. How does this story of Robin Hood end?

**Exercise 104 – Retelling the Story** (pages 24–28)

*See the instructions for Exercise 16. Do at least one topic as written work!*

1. Robin and Sir Guy (24,25–25,17)
2. Fighting the Sheriff's Men (25,21–26,14)
3. Buffets (26,20–28,12)
4. The Return of the King (28,12–28,35)

**Exercise 105 – Retelling: Grand Finale** (Chapters 1–7)

*How much of the story can you remember? Here your whole group can work on one topic, collecting points together, or perhaps some of you can choose topics individually and speak five, eight or ten sentences with no text in front of you.*
*If you do re-read a page, then don't spend longer than five minutes or so looking at it.*

1. At the Church and After (Chapter 1)
2. The Clearing and the Promise (Chapter 1)
3. Robin and Little John (Chapter 2)
4. The Archery Contest (Chapter3 )
5. Friar Tuck (Chapter 4)
6. Fighting the Friar (Chapter 4)
7. Food and Drink in Sherwood (Chapter 4)
8. The Bishop's Meal (Chapter 5)
9. Nottingham Market (Chapter 6)
10. Two Fights in the Forest (Chapter 7)
11. Pilgrim and King! (Chapter 7)
12. Half a Wedding and a Whole Wedding (Chapters 1 and 7)

# List of English Irregular Verbs

**Introduction**

*Here is a list of the most important irregular verbs in English. They are not arranged alphabetically, but in 'sound families', as experience has shown this to facilitate learning. Most classes will aim to have achieved an excellent knowledge, both oral and written, of the whole list by the end of Class 8; at earlier stages, selection of what is to be learned is a matter for the individual teacher.*

*Offering the complete list here, then, enables the teacher to select according to the specific needs of the class, while at the same time giving each pupil an overview of the material to be covered in the course of the Middle School.*

*The 85 irregular verbs occurring in the main text of this reader are marked with an asterisk (*) before the verb number.*

| | | | | | |
|---|---|---|---|---|---|
| GROUP 1 – BEGIN | | | | | |
| * | 1. | to begin | began | begun | anfangen |
| * | 2. | to spring | sprang | sprung | (plötzlich) springen |
| * | 3. | to sing | sang | sung | singen |
| * | 4. | to ring | rang | rung | läuten, anrufen |
| * | 5. | to swim | swam | swum | schwimmen |
| * | 6. | to drink | drank | drunk | trinken |
| | 7. | to sink | sank | sunk | sinken, versenken |
| | 8. | to stink | stank | stunk | stinken |
| GROUP 2 – CLING | | | | | |
| | 9. | to cling | clung | clung | s. klammern, festhalten |
| | 10. | to sting | stung | stung | stechen |
| | 11. | to fling | flung | flung | schleudern |
| * | 12. | to swing | swung | swung | schwingen, schwenken; baumeln |
| | 13. | to wring | wrung | wrung | (aus-)wringen |
| * | 14. | to hang | hung | hung | (auf-)hängen |
| | | | (hanged = henkte; erhängt!) | | |
| | 15. | to spin | spun | spun | s. drehen; *(Garn)* spinnen |
| | 16. | to dig | dug | dug | graben |
| | 17. | to stick | stuck | stuck | (an-)stecken, ankleben |
| * | 18. | to strike | struck | struck | schlagen, treffen |
| * | 19. | to win | won | won | gewinnen |
| GROUP 3 – SLEEP | | | | | |
| * | 20. | to sleep | slept | slept | schlafen |
| | 21. | to creep | crept | crept | kriechen |
| | 22. | to sweep | swept | swept | fegen, kehren |

| | | | | |
|---|---|---|---|---|
| * 23. | to keep | kept | kept | behalten |
| 24. | to weep | wept | wept | weinen |
| * 25. | to meet | met | met | treffen, begegnen |
| * 26. | to feel | felt | felt | (s.) fühlen |
| * 27. | to kneel | knelt | knelt | knien |
| 28. | to bleed | bled | bled | bluten |
| * 29. | to feed | fed | fed | füttern |
| * 30. | to flee | fled | fled | fliehen |
| * 31. | to lead | led | led | führen |
| * 32. | to leave | left | left | weggehen, verlassen |
| * 33. | to hold | held | held | halten |
| 34. | to deal | dealt | dealt | handeln, s. befassen mit |
| * 35. | to mean | meant | meant | bedeuten |
| 36. | to lean | leant | leant | (s.) lehnen |
| 37. | to dream | dreamt | dreamt | träumen |
| 38. | to read | read | read | lesen |

GROUP 4 – LEARN (ALLE VERBEN DIESER GRUPPE GEHEN AUCH MIT -ED STATT MIT -T!)

| | | | | |
|---|---|---|---|---|
| 39. | to burn | burnt (burned) | burnt (burned) | (ver-)brennen |
| * 40. | to learn | learnt (learned) | learnt (learned) | lernen |
| * 41. | to smell | smelt (smelled) | smelt (smelled) | riechen |
| 42. | to spell | spelt (spelled) | spelt (spelled) | buchstabieren |
| 43. | to spoil | spoilt (spoiled) | spoilt (spoiled) | verderben |
| 44. | to spill | spilt (spilled) | spilt (spilled) | verschütten |

GROUP 5 – SEND

| | | | | |
|---|---|---|---|---|
| 45. | to bend | bent | bent | biegen, beugen |
| * 46. | to lend | lent | lent | (ver-)leihen |
| * 47. | to send | sent | sent | schicken, senden |
| * 48. | to spend | spent | spent | *(Geld)* ausgeben; *(Zeit)* verbringen |
| 49. | to build | built | built | bauen |

GROUP 6 – FIND

| | | | | |
|---|---|---|---|---|
| * 50. | to find | found | found | finden |
| 51. | to bind | bound | bound | binden |
| 52. | to grind | ground | ground | mahlen; schleifen |
| 53. | to wind | wound | wound | winden |

GROUP 7 – THINK

| | | | | |
|---|---|---|---|---|
| * 54. | to buy | bought | bought | kaufen |
| * 55. | to bring | brought | brought | bringen |
| * 56. | to think | thought | thought | denken |
| * 57. | to fight | fought | fought | kämpfen |
| * 58. | to catch | c*au*ght | c*au*ght | fangen |
| 59. | to teach | t*au*ght | t*au*ght | lehren, unterrichten |

GROUP 8 – WRITE

| | | | | |
|---|---|---|---|---|
| * 60. | to drive | drove | driven | fahren; treiben; vertreiben |
| 61. | to rise | rose | risen | aufgehen *(Sonne);* s. erheben |
| 62. | to write | wrote | written | schreiben |
| * 63. | to ride | rode | ridden | reiten |

GROUP 9 – SHOOT

| | | | | |
|---|---|---|---|---|
| * 64. | to get | got | got | bekommen; werden |
| * 65. | to forget | forgot | forgotten | vergessen |
| * 66. | to shoot | shot | shot | schießen |
| * 67. | to shine | shone | shone | scheinen, glänzen |
| * 68. | to lose | lost | lost | verlieren |

GROUP 10 – SPEAK

| | | | | |
|---|---|---|---|---|
| * 69. | to speak | spoke | spoken | sprechen |
| * 70. | to steal | stole | stolen | stehlen |
| * 71. | to break | broke | broken | (zer-)brechen |
| 72. | to freeze | froze | frozen | frieren, gefrieren |
| 73. | to wake up | woke up | woken up | aufwachen; -wecken |
| * 74. | to tell | told | told | erzählen, sagen |
| * 75. | to sell | sold | sold | verkaufen |
| 76. | to choose | chose | chosen | (aus-)wählen |

GROUP 11 – WEAR

| | | | | |
|---|---|---|---|---|
| * 77. | to wear | wore | worn | *(Kleider)* tragen |
| 78. | to tear | tore | torn | zerreißen |
| 79. | to swear | swore | sworn | schwören, fluchen |
| 80. | to bear | bore | borne<br>(born = geboren!) | ertragen |

GROUP 12 – HIDE

| | | | | |
|---|---|---|---|---|
| * 81. | to hide | hid | hidden | (s.) verstecken |
| 82. | to bite | bit | bitten | beißen |
| * 83. | to light | lit (lighted) | lit (lighted) | anzünden |
| 84. | to slide | slid | slid | gleiten, rutschen |

GROUP 13 – 'W' VERBS

| | | | | |
|---|---|---|---|---|
| * 85. | to know | knew | known | kennen, wissen |
| * 86. | to blow | blew | blown | wehen, blasen |
| * 87. | to grow | grew | grown | wachsen; werden |
| * 88. | to throw | threw | thrown | werfen |
| * 89. | to fly | flew | flown | fliegen |
| * 90. | to draw | drew | drawn | zeichnen; ziehen |
| * 91. | to show | showed | shown | zeigen |
| 92. | to sow | sowed | sown | säen |
| 93. | to sew | sewed | sewn | nähen |
| 94. | to saw | sawed | sawn | sägen |

GROUP 14 – CUT

| | | | | |
|---|---|---|---|---|
| 95. | to bet | bet | bet | wetten |
| 96. | to broadcast | broadcast | broadcast | senden, ausstrahlen *(Radio/TV)* |
| * 97. | to burst | burst | burst | bersten, platzen |
| 98. | to cost | cost | cost | kosten |
| * 99. | to cut | cut | cut | schneiden |
| *100. | to hit | hit | hit | treffen, schlagen |
| *101. | to hurt | hurt | hurt | weh tun; verletzen |
| *102. | to let | let | let | (zu-)lassen |
| *103. | to put | put | put | stellen, setzen, legen |
| *104. | to set | set | set | setzen; untergehen *(Sonne)* |
| 105. | to shut | shut | shut | schließen |
| 106. | to spread | spread | spread | ausbreiten, ausdehnen; *(aufs Brot)* streichen |
| *107. | to thrust | thrust | thrust | stoßen |

GROUP 15 – AUXILIARY VERBS

| | | | | |
|---|---|---|---|---|
| *108. | to be | was / were | been | sein |
| *109. | to have | had | had | haben |
| *110. | to do | did | done | tun |

GROUP 16 – REMAINING VERBS

| | | | | |
|---|---|---|---|---|
| *111. | to make | made | made | machen |
| *112. | to go | went | gone | gehen, fahren |
| *113. | to come | came | come | kommen |
| *114. | to become | became | become | werden |
| *115. | to run | ran | run | laufen, rennen |
| *116. | to see | saw | seen | sehen |
| *117. | to hear | heard | heard | hören |
| *118. | to give | gave | given | geben |
| *119. | to forgive | forgave | forgiven | vergeben |
| 120. | to forbid | forbade | forbidden | verbieten |
| *121. | to say | said | said | sagen |
| *122. | to pay | paid | paid | bezahlen |
| *123. | to lay | laid | laid | legen |
| *124. | to lie | lay | lain | liegen |
| *125. | to sit | sat | sat | sitzen |
| *126. | to stand | stood | stood | stehen |
| 127. | to understand | understood | understood | verstehen |
| *128. | to beat | beat | beaten | schlagen |
| *129. | to take | took | taken | nehmen |
| *130. | to shake | shook | shaken | schütteln |
| *131. | to eat | ate | eaten | essen |
| *132. | to fall | fell | fallen | fallen |

## Epilogue

“ *Somewhere near Bolsover, in the 1820s, two pitmen were sinking a shaft for a new coalmine. Suddenly, the side of the shaft gave way, and there in front of them was a cave – but not an empty one! They saw a fireplace with an iron pot. They saw a blacksmith's shop, a kitchen full of pots and pans, a sick bay with its herbs and bandages, a storeroom full of sacks and barrels. And a rack of bows and quivers full of arrows. At the end of the gallery was a tiny chapel with the cross still on the altar.*

*The two pitmen stood staring like men in a dream. What was it they had found? At last, they saw a skeleton lying at the foot of a flat piece of wall, one hand holding a crucifix. Scratched on the cavern wall they saw a long list of names. At the top were the words* 'These died that we might live. Requiescant in pace,' *and at the bottom,* 'I was the last. Michael Tuck.'

*The skeleton was Friar Tuck's. He had scratched these last few words before he died.*

*The two pitmen were now very nervous. But one thing they were certain of. They must run and tell the nearest clergyman or schoolmaster and bring them here to see it. Such people would be able to explain.*

*But they had barely reached the top of the shaft, when there came a great rockfall, thundering downwards, some of the smaller stones only just missing them as they ran. Everything that had been there before was buried under hundreds of tons of rock.*

*When they told their story in the village no one would believe them. People had heard the rocks rumbling and had seen the cloud of dust. But that sort of thing often happened and they only laughed when the pitmen tried to describe what they had seen.*

*Soon the pitmen themselves began to wonder whether it had not been a sort of dream. And in time they both died and the secret was lost.*

*I am sure that what they had seen was truly Robin Hood's cave, just as he and the outlaws had left it. The two pitmen were the last ever to see it. But it is still there, only a little way below the ground close to a worked-out pit. One fine day it will be found again. I wonder who will find it!* ”

From: *Robin Hood – His Life and Legend* by Bernard Miles (Abridged & adapted)